THE *Church History* OF
RUFINUS OF AQUILEIA
BOOKS 10 AND 11

THE *Church History* OF
RUFINUS OF AQUILEIA

BOOKS 10 AND 11

*Translated by*
Philip R. Amidon, S.J.

*New York    Oxford • Oxford University Press    1997*

Oxford University Press

Oxford   New York

Athens   Auckland   Bangkok   Bogota   Bombay   Buenos Aires
Calcutta   Cape Town   Dar es Salaam   Delhi   Florence   Hong Kong
Istanbul   Karachi   Kuala Lumpur   Madras   Madrid   Melbourne
Mexico City   Nairobi   Paris   Singapore   Taipei   Tokyo   Toronto   Warsaw

and associated companies in
Berlin   Ibadan

Copyright © 1997 by Philip R. Amidon

Published by Oxford University Press
198 Madison Avenue, New York, New York 10016

Oxford is a registered trademark of Oxford University Press

Library of Congress Cataloging-in-Publication Data
Rufinus, of Aquileia, 345–410.
The church history of Rufinus of Aquileia, books 10 and 11
translated by Philip R. Amidon.
p.   cm.
The author's continuation to his translation of: Ecclesiastical
history / Eusebius, of Caesarea, Bishop of Caesarea.
Includes bibliographical references.
ISBN 0-19-511031-5
1. Church history—Primitive and early church, ca. 30–600.
I. Amidon, Philip R.   II. Eusebius, of Caesarea, Bishop of Caesarea,
ca. 260–ca. 340.   Ecclesiastical history.   III. Title.
BR160.R8E54   1997
270.2—dc20        96-41365

1 3 5 7 9 8 6 4 2

Printed in the United States of America
on acid-free paper

# CONTENTS

*Introduction*   VII

The *Church History* of Rufinus of Aquileia   1

Preface of Rufinus to the History of Eusebius   3

Preface of Rufinus to the Continuation   5

Book 10   7

Book 11   61

*Abbreviations*   115

*Bibliography*   117

*Index of Names*   125

# INTRODUCTION

What is known of the life of Tyrannius (or Turranius) Rufinus is well set out in F. X. Murphy's authoritative biography.[1] He was born around 345 C.E. in Iulia Concordia (west of Aquileia). His parents were noble and wealthy, to judge from his education, which he completed in Rome. While a student there he became close friends with Jerome.

Athanasius had popularized monasticism in the West during his long exile there, a year of which was spent in Aquileia around the time of Rufinus's birth. By 370 there was an ascetic community in Aquileia that Rufinus joined upon his return from Rome. He was baptized in 369 or 370. His enthusiasm for the monastic life inspired him, as it did other Western Christians, to visit its birthplace, and he made his way to Egypt at the end of 372 or early in 373.

It was about the same time, in November of 372, that Antonia Melania, a widow of the highest nobility who had likewise taken up the ascetic life, sailed from Rome to the East. She arrived in Alexandria at about the same time as Rufinus (although there is no reason to suppose that they traveled together), just in time to witness the outbreak of the Arian persecution that followed Athanasius's death (in May of 373). She decided to follow a group of exiles from the persecution to Diocaesarea in Palestine, and from there went on to Jerusalem in 375.

Rufinus, meanwhile, stayed in Egypt to continue his studies for six years under Didymus the Blind and others; it was Didymus who introduced him to Origen's works. He spent 378(?) visiting the other homeland of monasticism, in Palestine and Syria, and then returned to Alexandria for a final two years of study with Didymus.

Melania, meanwhile, had founded a monastery in Jerusalem, where Rufinus joined her perhaps in 380. It was a double monastery, for women and men, the first such Latin foundation in the Holy Land, and it included a guest house for pilgrims. Rufinus, in his part of the monastery, directed the copying of books (including the Latin classics, for which there would have been some demand in the new Latin colonies of the Near East). He must have been ordained presbyter about this time.

Jerome arrived in 385 to tour the Near East, and in 386 his friend Paula began work on a double monastery in Bethlehem after the example of Melania and Rufinus. His relationship with Rufinus, however, cooled for a number of reasons,[2] until it was finally disrupted by the outbreak of the Origenist controversy. Both of them had admired Origen greatly, but Epiphanius of Salamis's attempt (in 393) to get John of Jerusalem to condemn Origen as the forerunner of Arius drew different responses from them. Rufinus followed John in refusing to do so, while Jerome agreed to the condemnation. The two of them, together with their monks, were divided over the issue, which dragged on for years. Jerome and Rufinus were finally reconciled in 397, the same year Rufinus returned to Italy, taking his books with him.

He found, when he landed in Rome, that rumor of the Origenist quarrel had far outrun him. It was not long before he was asked to translate Pamphilus's *Vindication of Origen*. To it he added his own *The Falsification of Origen's Works*, in which he explained that the heterodox views found in Origen's books were the falsifications and interpolations of his enemies.

He spent the fall of 397 and spring of 398 at the monastery of Pinetum, near Terracina, where he translated Basil's *Rules* for Abbot Ursacius. It was also in 398 that at the instance of the noble scholar Macarius he undertook his fateful translation of Origen's *First Prin-*

*ciples.* In his preface he repeated his view that the text had been corrupted by Origen's enemies, and he explained that he had therefore altered or replaced statements of doubtful orthodoxy with other, sounder ones taken from Origen's other works. He also said that in doing so he was simply following Jerome's lead, both in translating Origen into Latin and in suppressing suspect passages in him (he did not mention him by name but alluded to him so clearly that the reference was unmistakable). Word of his project got around Rome, and the anti-Origenist party denounced him and complained to Jerome.

His translation of the letter to St. James the Apostle attributed to Clement of Rome may perhaps also be dated to around this time, but by the second half of 398 Rufinus had had enough of the Origenist controversy; he left Rome for the more peaceful atmosphere of Aquileia after writing Jerome an apparently amicable letter explaining his move. Jerome, meanwhile, stung by his friend's public reminder of his own earlier infatuation with Origen, made a literal translation of the *First Principles* and sent it to Rome, together with an angry open letter to his friends there in which he practically accused Rufinus's translation of fostering heresy. He also wrote a private letter to Rufinus explaining the apologetic purpose of the open letter; he evidently hoped to avoid a public break. But Jerome's friends in Rome withheld the letter from Rufinus and drummed up a campaign against him throughout Italy.

Once settled in Aquileia, Rufinus continued producing translations: of Basil's homilies and Gregory's discourses, the *Sentences of Sextus*, Adamantius's *De recta in Deum fide*, the *Commentary on the Apostles' Creed*, and Origen on Joshua, Judges, and Psalms 36–38.

Pope Siricius died in November of 399 and was succeeded by Anastasius, who proved more sympathetic to Rufinus's anti-Origenist foes. Theophilus of Alexandria now took the field against Origen, presiding over a council which condemned him in 400. The emperor confirmed its sentence and proscribed Origen's works; Theophilus communicated this in a letter to Anastasius. The pope in turn confirmed the council's sentence and communicated his decision to Simplician of Milan, inviting him and his colleagues in northern Italy to add their own confirmation. But Simplician died that year, so Anastasius wrote to his successor Venerius repeating his invitation. Rufinus, by now feeling himself under increasing pressure, composed the *Apology to Anastasius*. Anastasius made no direct answer, but to John of Jerusalem, who had expressed concern about his old friend, he replied condemning Origen but adding that he wished to know nothing about Rufinus, neither where he was nor what he was about.

Rufinus, worried and resentful at having received no reply to his letter to Jerome (as he thought), replied to Jerome's criticisms in 401 with his *Apology against Jerome*. In it he defended himself against the imputation of heresy and furnished massive evidence of Jerome's own earlier devotion not only to Origen's exegesis but to his speculative theology as well. It was the final break; Jerome replied the same year with his ferocious *Apology against Rufinus*, and although the latter, after one final personal letter, discontinued the public argument thereafter, Jerome pursued him with vitriolic pen even beyond the grave, much to Augustine's dismay.

It was in November of this year that Alaric and his Goths marched into Italy and in 402 laid siege to Milan. With his city under threat, Chromatius of Aquileia asked Rufinus to translate Eusebius of Caesarea's *Church History*, the reading of which he thought might divert his people's attention from their danger. Eusebius's work had, since its publication in 325, acquired an extensive and well-deserved reputation for its learned and edifying survey of Christian history from its beginning to the end of the pagan persecutions. Rufinus agreed to Chromatius's request and in 402 or 403 published an abridged translation of the original, together with his own continuation of it to carry it forward to the year 395 (the date of Theodosius's death).

By then the Gothic threat had receded, and Rufinus may well have left Aquileia for Rome at this time; he was almost certainly there by the middle of 406 and probably earlier. The atmosphere there had become more congenial to him since the return of his powerful patroness Melania in 400, the succession of Innocent I in 402 following the death of Anastasius, and the new antipathy many people felt for the anti-Origenist party due to the exile of John Chrysostom, the most celebrated victim of Theophilus's campaign against the Origenist monks. It cannot be proved beyond all objection that he left Aquileia before 407, but the circumstantial evidence is strong.[3] The years 403–406, at any rate, saw him back at work on translations of Origen: his commentaries on Genesis, Exodus, and Leviticus, and the Letter to the Romans. He also translated the *History of the Monks in Egypt*, perhaps as a contribution to the campaign in favor of John Chrysostom, and the pseudo-Clementine *Recognitions*. Pelagius, also in Rome at this time, was put into fateful contact with Origen through his translations. He laid Origen/Rufinus under heavy tribute in forming his own doctrine on free will and grace, being influenced in particular by the Commentary on Romans.

The Elder Melania left Italy to return to the Holy Land in 406 or early 407. Rufinus also thought of returning there, but for some reason he put it off, and in 408 he was forced to join the great caravan of his fellow Romans fleeing to Sicily before a new invasion of Goths. There, from across the strait, he watched Rhegium go up in flames under Alaric's assault, and there he died in 410 or 411, still at work translating (Origen on Song of Songs, I Samuel, Numbers, and perhaps Deuteronomy).[4]

Rufinus was a person of unquestionable importance in the turbulent history of the church in the late fourth and early fifth centuries. He can hardly match Jerome's colorful personality and brilliant style, but together with him he introduced the Latin-speaking church to a trove of important Greek Christian literature that had hitherto been practically inaccessible to it. He had little of the other's acuteness in exegesis, but he had an equally thorough mastery of Greek and a better sense of historiography.[5]

Whatever may have been his at least professed initial hesitation in acceding to Chromatius's request for a translation of Eusebius's *Church History*, his execution of the project shows a keen appreciation of the narrative power of the original, clumsily dressed though it was in the author's infelicitous style. It is true that he translated freely, at times to the point of paraphrasing. But he viewed the history of the church of his own time as a reproduction in miniature of the vast canvas of the first centuries of its life painted by Eusebius, on which the pattern of mission, persecution, division, and salvation stood out so clearly. Just as the earliest church in its deprivation and suffering, the seedbed of its mission, had been aided by God's power working through His servants and been securely established by the pious emperor Constantine, so that of his own time had seen God's power equally at work in the lives of its

holy ones to extend its mission in the midst of suffering and to reestab-
lish its safety with the accession of the orthodox emperor Theodosius.
The reproduction was not exact, for this time most of the persecutors
were Christian (and therefore much more dangerous). But for Rufinus,
this is the secret of church history: the power of God revealed in weakness. The weakness is evidenced in persecutions and in the divisions of
heresy and schism, but the power shows forth in the lives of holy Christians through whom God continues to work the kind of wonders recorded in previous times in the Scriptures. For Rufinus there is but one
people of God, with one continuous history in which this pattern is
revealed. That is what he set out to offer the Western Church in his
translation and continuation.[6]

His history was an instant and lasting success. It was the first Latin
Christian history and, as such, exerted great influence over both his
contemporaries and later generations. Augustine relied on it in composing the historical sections of the *City of God*. Paul Orosius implic-
itly challenged its outlook in his *Historiae adversus paganos* (417). But the
Byzantine church historians Socrates and Sozomen as well were deeply
(and not always happily) influenced by it; Socrates (at least) evidently
read it in the original Latin. He later had to rewrite the first two books
of his history in order to correct Rufinus's chronology. He continued
to use him nonetheless, and his and Sozomen's works won for Rufinus
a place among the few Latin Christians to affect the course of Greek
Christian literature. Even more important, perhaps, was his influence
in the later Western Church right through the Middle Ages, when
Greek was forgotten and his translation/continuation offered it the
only available view of its earliest formative history.

In the prefaces to the translation and to the continuation, Rufinus
distinguishes between the methods he used in the two. He says that
he shortened Eusebius's original as he saw fit. In fact, he abridged freely
and often drastically, smoothing out inconsistencies and irrelevancies
(as he saw them), simplifying the style, and expunging any tinges of
heterodoxy (about which he was by this time quite sensitive). "He felt
himself justified in replacing imprecise words and phrases in Eusebius
with expressions which were clear and unambiguous. Nor did [he]
hesitate to rewrite or add explanations of his own if this would aid
understanding."[7] He also occasionally added items from his own ex-

perience. His additions to the martyrdom accounts square with the extant Acts and show that he took the trouble to consult documents for fuller information.[8]

For the continuation of the history, Rufinus says that he relied upon records and his own memory: "on what has come down from those before us, and . . . on what we remembered," as the preface to the translation puts it, or as he repeats in the preface to the continuation, "[the material that] we either found in the writings of those before us or we remembered." But here we come upon the controversy surrounding his relationship with the first continuer of Eusebius's history: Gelasius of Caesarea.

In his influential monograph of 1914,[9] Anton Glas noted that Greek texts paralleling most of Rufinus's continuation can be assembled from Gelasius of Cyzicus's *Syntagma* (fifth century) and from the *Chronicle* of George the Monk (ninth century). But the passages where Gelasius explicitly cites Rufinus are not in fact from him; they deal with a time before his continuation begins. As for George, he was (all agree) incapable of translating Latin (at least into the kind of Greek where he parallels Rufinus). Nor did he copy from the *Syntagma*; much of his text is not found there, and even where their texts run parallel in content, one is not a copy of the other. From this Glas inferred that there existed a Greek history which early became attributed to Rufinus for some reason. Now the *Syntagma* in one place (1.8.1) refers to "Rufinus or Gelasius" as a source. Glas therefore concluded that Rufinus's continuation had at some point become confused with that of Gelasius of Caesarea (well attested but long since vanished). The independence of Gelasius's is shown both by the fact that it began before Rufinus's and by a comparison of passages where its Greek is preserved: Rufinus's is clearly a translation of the other. Therefore, whatever he may have claimed in his prefaces, Rufinus did little more in his continuation than translate Gelasius without attribution.

In the following year Paul van den Ven independently suggested the existence of a Greek version of Rufinus's continuation, attributed to Gelasius of Caesarea, from which later sources drew.[10] He wrote without reference to Glas, but his article was viewed as a defense of Rufinus's honor, and from then on the battle lines between German- and French-language scholarship were drawn up in almost perfect order.

In 1932 Peter Heseler, accepting Glas's conclusions without discussion, presented as excerpts from Gelasius of Caesarea texts from the *Life of Metrophanes and Alexander* and the *Life of Constantine and Helena*.[11]

In 1938 Franz Diekamp, in the only German-language article to oppose Glas's thesis overall, protested that a comparison of Rufinus's Latin with the parallel Greek passages would not yield more securely the conclusion that the Latin was a translation than the converse.[12] It might be true that he had translated the *History of the Monks in Egypt* without attribution and that his commentary on the creed depended in great part on Cyril of Jerusalem's *Catecheses*, but in the former case he simply translated an anonymous work anonymously, while in the introduction to the latter he admitted his debt to others. Thus neither case proves that his claim to independent authorship in the preface to his continuation should not be taken seriously.

In 1946 Van den Ven published his agreement with Diekamp: Rufinus's work was the original, and Gelasius had translated him with additions of his own.[13]

Felix Scheidweiler came to Glas's defense in 1953, rejecting Diekamp's attempt to save Rufinus's integrity.[14] Rufinus's continuation, whatever he claimed, was mainly a translation of Gelasius's with a few additions of his own. The reason that the credit later went to Rufinus was that both Socrates and Gelasius of Cyzicus cite him as a source, and their later readers, noticing the parallels between Rufinus and Gelasius of Caesarea, must have assumed, on Socrates' authority, that Rufinus was the original whom he had consulted. But Rufinus's text bears all the earmarks of translation, in contrast to the Greek parallels.

Ernest Honigmann advanced the debate the following year with the observation that according to the address of Letter 92 in Jerome's collection, Gelasius of Caesarea must have died in or before the year 400. Thus his work is independent of Rufinus's, which was published afterward. But later readers of Gelasius of Cyzicus may have been misled by his claim that Rufinus attended the Council of Nicaea (*Syntagma*, Proem. 1.21–22) and may have thought of Rufinus as older than Gelasius of Caesarea. They may also have thought that he wrote only of that council, if all that they knew of his work came from Gelasius of Cyzicus. Honigmann proposed that someone during the fifth century composed a kind of *historia bipartita* or *tripartita* in Greek covering the Council of

Nicaea or perhaps the reigns of Constantius Chlorus and Constantine. It may have borne a title which made readers think that Rufinus and Gelasius were the same person. That would explain why passages not in the Latin Rufinus were later attributed to him. He also conjectured that during this period there was as well a Greek text corresponding closely to the Latin Rufinus; perhaps Rufinus himself composed it. He did admit that Rufinus had probably used Gelasius's history.[15]

Scheidweiler welcomed Honigmann's proof of Gelasius of Caesarea's priority, but rejected his hypothesis about a "Greek Rufinus." Rufinus remained for him little more than the translator of Gelasius's history.[16]

In 1962 Ernest Bihain made the little noticed but useful suggestion that attention be paid to how Cyril of Jerusalem, Gelasius of Caesarea's uncle and patron, shows up in passages supposedly deriving from his nephew, as in the critical notice in Socrates 2.38.2.[17]

In a series of publications from 1964 to 1982, Friedhelm Winkelmann surveyed the ground gained and yielded by either side in the debate. The priority and therefore independence of Gelasius of Caesarea's history had been established, but not its extension; though two of the ancient sources mentioned that it reached back into Diocletian's reign,[18] none of them said how far forward in time it extended. If one assumed that Rufinus had done little more than translate Gelasius, then the latter must have been the original author of the lengthy narratives of events in Egypt which take up so much of Rufinus's Book 11. But it was Rufinus who spent years in Egypt and who could be supposed to have had firsthand knowledge of what had happened there; Gelasius may never have visited it. Winkelmann accepted this point, and he also disagreed with Scheidweiler that Rufinus's Latin looked like a translation. He did, however, agree with him that it was Gelasius who had moved the Council of Tyre which condemned Athanasius to Constantius's reign; Rufinus had merely followed his chronology. All things considered, then, he marked Rufinus's Book 10.1–15 as certainly an abridged and slightly modified translation of Gelasius, and he thought the same could probably be said of the following chapters up to and including 11.3 (about half to two-thirds of the whole). As for Socrates' complaint about having to revise and correct Rufinus's chronology, Winkelmann boldly claimed that Socrates was telling an untruth; it was really Gelasius he had been using for his first draft. And as for the difficult fact that there are Greek parallel texts to Rufinus even after 11.3, from which point he is certainly the original author, Winkelmann hypothesized that someone had translated him into Greek from the point where Gelasius left off, in order to provide a continuous Greek church history down to the death of Theodosius. But a careful study of the topography of Rufinus's history could, he thought, make possible the exhumation of at least the skeleton of Gelasius's.[19]

In 1987, however, Jacques Schamp cancelled the exhumation order after a close study of Photius's remarks about Gelasius of Caesarea, in which he argued persuasively that according to the patriarch, not only did his history end with Arius's death, but it placed that death (in contrast to Rufinus) in Constantine's reign.[20] Both observations reduce the possible extent of Rufinus's dependence on Gelasius to the point where all hope of using the Latin history to reconstruct the Greek one vanishes.

Françoise Thelamon, meanwhile, in the introduction to her magistral study of Rufinus, *Païens et chrétiens au IVᵉ siècle* (Paris, 1981), dismissed the whole discussion as a misguided attempt to compare a still extant work with one now entirely lost, and she proceeded to treat Rufinus's history as an original work.[21]

The results of the debate may be summed up as follows. Gelasius of Caesarea certainly wrote a continuation to Eusebius's *Church History*, and he certainly completed it before Rufinus set to work on his; the ancient authorities leave no doubt on either point. It apparently began with Diocletian's reign and ended with the death of Arius. Rufinus probably consulted it and may have translated or paraphrased some passages without attribution. The conventions of his day were different from ours; as Manlio Simonetti remarks, "The custom of publishing under one's own name works which were essentially nothing more than paraphrases of Greek originals was by then wide-spread in the Christian world,"[22] and both Jerome and Rufinus engaged in this activity.

Schamp's investigations, however, show that this is not the way he used Gelasius, whose history ended with Arius's death in 335. Rufinus's own work continued on to the death of Theodosius in 395. He does not name his other sources, so we cannot tell how he employed them.

But as Thelamon has so clearly shown, he wrote according to a definite plan; however deeply he drew from his sources, the final arrangement and form of his history are his own.

The hypothesis, put forward by various parties on either side of the debate, of a Greek translation of Rufinus's continuation, seems to have gained widespread acceptance. The influence he exercised upon the course of Greek church history through the lawyer-historians who could read him in the original is already considerable, but a Greek translation would have extended that influence immeasurably.

His work has been variously assessed over the past century. By modern historical standards it fares badly when compared with Eusebius's *Church History*, which is impressive in its discrimination of sources and nothing short of revolutionary in its citation of them. The revolution does not continue in Rufinus. He does not name his sources, with one or two exceptions, and he shows little of Eusebius's wariness of miraculous tales. He also displays in his continuation an almost unparalleled capacity for chronological errors, some of which appear to be deliberate. If judged by its purpose, however, which was to buck up the beleaguered faithful of Aquileia, it may be said to be "a competent piece of work, admirably suited to the purpose he had in mind. It certainly is a vivid, well-written narrative."[23] It may be added that the continuation is also of considerable importance as a source for ancient and modern scholarship alike. Great was his authority among the Byzantine historians (Gelasius of Cyzicus believed he had attended the Council of Nicaea in person, as we have seen), and he will often be found to be the first source for the events they record (and the origin of the errors they repeat).

Rufinus condensed the ten books of Eusebius's history into nine in translation, so that the additional two books of his continuation are entitled Books 10 and 11 in the Latin work as a whole. These are the two books that are translated here. This is the first English translation of them. There is also an Italian translation in the *Collana di testi patristici* series.[24] The Latin edition used is that of Theodor Mommsen in the *Griechische Christliche Schriftsteller* series.[25] Special mention must also be made of Thelamon's work, cited earlier; it has become the standard reference for all modern studies of Rufinus's continuation, and the extent to which the present commentary is indebted to it will be easily apparent.

NOTES TO INTRODUCTION

1. *Rufinus of Aquileia* (345–411): *His Life and Works* (Washington, 1945). See also C. P. Hammond's indispensable article, "The Last Ten Years of Rufinus' Life and the Date of His Move South from Aquileia," *JTS*, N.S., 28 (1977), 372–429. Cf. as well G. Fedalto, "Rufino di Concordia. Elementi di una biografia," *AAAd*, 39 (1992), 19–44.

2. Cf. J. N. D. Kelly, *Jerome* (New York, 1975), 196.

3. Cf. Hammond, "The Last Ten Years of Rufinus' Life," note 1.

4. Not all of Rufinus's works are covered here, and the dates of composition of many of them must remain conjectural. For a complete list cf. ibid., 428–429.

5. On Jerome's adaptation of Eusebius's *Chronicle*, see Kelly, *Jerome*, 72–75.

6. Cf. F. Thelamon, "Rufin historien de son temps," *AAAd*, 31 (1987), 1.41–59, and "Apôtres et prophètes de notre temps,'" *AAAd*, 39 (1992), 171–198.

7. T. Christensen, *Rufinus of Aquileia and the "Historia Ecclesiastica," Lib. VIII–IX, of Eusebius* (Copenhagen, 1989), 333.

8. J. E. L. Oulton, "Rufinus's Translation of the Church History of Eusebius," *JTS* 30 (1929), 150–174.

9. *Die Kirchengeschichte des Gelasios von Kaisareia* (*Byzantinisches Archiv* 6, 1914).

10. "Fragments de la recension grecque de l'histoire ecclésiastique de Rufin dans un texte hagiographique," *Le Muséon* 33 (1915), 92–105.

11. "Hagiographica I" and "Hagiographica II," *Byzantinisch-Neugriechische Jahrbücher* 9 (1932), 113–128 and 320–337.

12. "Gelasius von Caesarea in Palaestina," *Analecta Patristica* (*Orientalia Christiana Analecta* 117 [1938]), 16–49.

13. "Encore le Rufin grec," *Le Muséon* 59 (1946), 281–294.

14. "Die Kirchengeschichte des Gelasios von Kaisareia," *Byzantinische Zeitschrift* 46 (1953), 277–301.

15. "Gélase de Césarée et Rufin d'Aquilée," *Académie royale de Belgique. Bulletin de la classe des lettres et des sciences morales et politiques* 40 (1954), 122–161.

16. *Byzantinische Zeitschrift* 48 (1955), 162–164, and 50 (1957), 74–98 (critical reviews of Honigmann's article in note 15).

17. "La source d'un texte de Socrate (HE 2.38.2) relatif à Cyrille de Jérusalem," *Byzantion* 32 (1962), 81–91.

18. Cf. Honigmann, "Gélase de Césarée," 159–160.

19. "Das Problem der Rekonstruktion der Historia Ecclesiastica des Gelasius von Caesarea," *Forschungen und Fortschritte* 38 (1964), 311–314; *Untersuchungen zur Kirchengeschichte des Gelasios von Kaisareia* (*Sitzungsberichte der deutschen Akademie der Wissenschaften zu Berlin*, Klasse für Sprachen, Literatur und Kunst 1965.3); "Charakter und Bedeutung der Kirchengeschichte des Gelasios von Kaisareia," *Byzantinische Forschungen* 1 (1966), 346–385; "Die Quellen der Historia Ecclesiastica des Gelasios von Cyzicus (nach 475)," *Byzantinoslavica* 27 (1966), 104–130; "Zu einer Edition der Fragmente der Kirchengeschichte des Gelasios von Kaisareia," *Byzantinoslavica* 34 (1973), 193–198; "Vita Metrophanis et Alexandri," *Analecta Bollandiana* 100 (1982), 147–184.

20. "Gélase ou Rufin: un fait nouveau," *Byzantion* 57 (1987), 360–390; "The Lost Ecclesiastical History of Gelasius of Caesarea," *The Patristic and Byzantine Review* 6.2 (1987), 146–152.

21. Thelamon *PC* 20.

22. "L'attività letteraria di Rufino negli anni della controversia origeniana," *AAAd* 39 (1992), 91.

23. Murphy, *Rufinus of Aquileia*, 174.

24. L. Dattrino, *Rufino. Storia della chiesa* (Rome, 1986).

25. *Eusebius Werke* 2.2. *Die Kirchengeschichte*, ed. E. Schwartz and T. Mommsen (Leipzig, 1908).

THE *Church History* OF
RUFINUS OF AQUILEIA

BOOKS 10 AND 11

# PREFACE OF RUFINUS
## TO THE HISTORY
## OF EUSEBIUS

It is the business of skillful physicians, they say, to provide some sort of medicine or potion when they see that cities or regions are threatened by epidemics, so that people may be protected by it from the death that threatens them. This is the sort of medical art which you have practiced, my reverend father Chromatius,* at this time when the Goths have burst through the barriers into Italy with Alaric at their head, and a lethal plague is spreading far and wide, to the ruin of fields, herds, and men: you have sought some remedy to protect from cruel death the people God has entrusted to you, a remedy by which ailing spirits may be diverted from the thought of impending evil and give their attention to something better. Thus you have charged me to translate into Latin the church history which that most learned man Eusebius of Caesarea composed in Greek, that the attention of those who hear it may be occupied and they may for a while come to forget present evils while their interest is directed to the affairs of the past. At first I wanted to beg off the work as being unequal to it and as having lost fluency in Latin after so many years, but then it occurred to me that

*Bishop of Aquileia ca. 388–407 and Rufinus's patron.

3

what you had ordered me to do was not unrelated to apostolic tradition. On the occasion when the crowds of those listening to him were hungry in the desert, the Lord said to the apostles, "You give them something to eat." Philip, one of the apostles, realizing that the signs of divine power are clearer when they are accomplished by those who are least, did not bring out the loaves stored in the apostles' bag; rather, he said that there was a small boy there who had five loaves and two fish, adding apologetically in his regard, "But what are these among so many?," so that the divine power might be even more evident where the resources were hopelessly slim. Now I know that you stand in this very tradition, and it occurred to me that you might have followed Philip's example, when you saw that the crowds needed to be fed, and chosen a small boy who would not only produce the five loaves doubled, as he had received them, but would also, in fulfillment of the gospel mystery, add the two little fish caught by his own effort. I have therefore proceeded to carry out your order as well as I could, certain that our shortcomings would be excused on account of the authority of the one who issued it.

Now it should be noted that since the tenth book of this work in Greek has very little history in it, all the rest of it being taken up with bishops' panegyrics which add nothing to our knowledge of the facts, we have omitted what seemed superfluous and joined what history there was in it to the ninth book, which we have made the conclusion of Eusebius's account. The tenth and eleventh books we composed based partly on what has come down from those before us, and partly on what we remembered, adding them like two little fish to the aforesaid loaves. If you approve and bless them, I am certain that they will satisfy the crowds. Now the entire work treats the affairs of the church from the Savior's Ascension and after, while our two short books go from the time of Constantine after the persecution to the death of the emperor Theodosius.

# PREFACE OF RUFINUS TO THE CONTINUATION

The record of the affairs of the church with which Eusebius has provided us extends to this point. We for our part have briefly added, to the best of our ability, the events which followed in the course of time down to the present, and which we either found in the writings of those before us or we remembered, obedient as always to the injunctions of our father in religion.

# BOOK 10

1. The heresy of Arius.
2. The council which met in Nicaea.
3. The conversion of the dialectician.
4. The confessor Paphnutius.
5. Bishop Spyridon and his wonders.
6. A copy of the Creed and Decrees of Nicaea.
7. Helena, the mother of Constantine.
8. The Savior's cross found by Helena in Jerusalem.
9. The captivity of Frumentius and Aedesius.
10. The conversion of the Indians accomplished by them.
11. The conversion of the Georgians accomplished by a captive woman.
12. Constantia, Constantine's sister, and the presbyter introduced by her to her brother.
13. The struggle between Alexander, Eusebius, and Arius.
14. The shameful death of Arius.
15. The early years of Bishop Athanasius.
16. The error of the emperor Constantius.
17. The heretical council convened in Tyre against Athanasius.
18. Arsenius's amputated arm and the other tricks of the heretics discovered at the council.

19. The flight and concealment of Athanasius.

20. How the emperor Constans wrote on behalf of Athanasius to his brother Constantius and ordered him to be restored to his church.

21. The council held in Milan and the exiles of Eusebius, Lucifer, and the other Catholic bishops.

22. The Council of Ariminum.

23. Liberius, bishop of Rome.

24. The bishops of Jerusalem and Alexandria.

25. The confusion of bishops in Antioch.

26. The schism of the Arians, who were divided into three parties: some were Eunomians, others Macedonians, and others remained Arians.

27. The death of the emperor Constantius and the rise of Julian.

28. The bishops released from exile.

29. The council of the holy bishops in Alexandria and Lucifer's separation from them.

30. The decrees formulated in that council.

31. Eusebius and Hilary and the restoration of the churches accomplished by them.

32. The writings of Hilary.

33. Julian's seductive and ingenious persecutions.

34. His cruelty toward Bishop Athanasius.

35. Athanasius's renewed flight and concealment.

36. The tomb of the martyr Babylas.

37. The confessor Theodore in Antioch.

38. The activities of the Jews who, deceived by Julian, undertook the restoration of the temple in Jerusalem.

39. How the Jews were deterred from their lawless project by an earthquake there and by a fire divinely kindled.

40. The signs and terrifying miracles which resulted in the death of the Jews.

10.1. Alexander received the episcopal office after Achillas, who had succeeded the martyr Peter in Alexandria, and it was then that since our people were enjoying peace and a respite from persecution, and the glory of the churches was crowned by the merits of the confessors, the favorable state of our affairs was disturbed by strife within. A presbyter of Alexandria named Arius, a man religious in appearance and aspect rather than in virtue, but shamefully desirous of glory, praise, and novelties, began to propose certain impious doctrines regarding the faith of Christ, things which had never before been talked about. He tried to sever and divide the Son from the eternal and ineffable substance or nature of God the Father, something which upset very many in the church. Bishop Alexander, by nature gentle and reserved, desired to recall Arius from his impious enterprise and teaching by unceasing admonitions, but did not succeed, because by then the contagion of his pestilential doctrine had infected so many not only in Alexandria, but also in the other cities and provinces to which it had spread. He therefore, thinking it would be disastrous to ignore the situation, brought it to the notice of very many of his fellow priests.[1] The dispute became widely known. Word of it reached the ears of the religious sovereign, since he was making every effort to look after our affairs. He then, in accordance with the mind of the priests, summoned a council of bishops to the city of Nicaea, and ordered Arius to present himself there to the 318 bishops in attendance and to be judged on the teachings and questions he had brought forward.[2]

10.2. Now I do not think it right to omit the marvelous thing which the sovereign did in the council. For when the bishops had come together from almost everywhere and, as usually happens, were submitting complaints against each other arising from various causes, he was constantly being importuned by each of them, petitions were being offered, wrongdoings were being brought up, and they were giving their attention to these matters rather than to the purpose of their gathering. But he, seeing that these quarrels were hindering the most important business at hand, set a certain day on which any bishop who thought he had a complaint to make might submit it. And when he had taken his seat, he accepted the petitions of each. Holding all the petitions together in his lap, and not opening them to see what they contained, he said to the bishops, "God has appointed you priests and given you power to judge even concerning us, and therefore we are rightly judged by you, while you cannot be judged by men. For this reason, wait for God alone to judge among you, and whatever your quarrels may be, let them be saved for that divine scrutiny. For you have been given to us by God as gods, and it is not fitting that a man should judge gods, but only he of whom it is written: God has stood in the assembly of the gods, in the midst he has judged between gods.[3] And therefore put aside these matters and without contention examine those things which belong to the faith of God." Having spoken thus, he ordered all the petitions containing complaints to be burned together, lest the dissension between priests become known to anyone. Now when the issue concerning faith had been discussed in the bishops' council for many days, and quite a few there put forward different views and vigorously supported Arius's initiative, there were still more who abhorred the impious enterprise. And since there were at the council a large number of priest-confessors, they were all opposed to Arius's novelties. But those who supported him were men clever in disputation and therefore opposed to the simplicity of faith.

**10.3.** Now we may learn how much power there is in simplicity of faith from what is reported to have happened there. For when the zeal of the religious emperor had brought together priests of God from all over the earth, rumor of the event gathered as well philosophers and dialecticians of great renown and fame. One of them who was celebrated for his ability in dialectic used to hold ardent debates each day with our bishops, men likewise by no means unskilled in the art of disputation, and there resulted a magnificent display for the learned and educated men who gathered to listen. Nor could the philosopher be cornered or trapped in any way by anyone, for he met the questions proposed with such rhetorical skill that whenever he seemed most firmly trapped, he escaped like a slippery snake. But that God might show that the kingdom of God is based upon power rather than speech, one of the confessors, a man of the simplest character who knew only Christ Jesus and him crucified,[4] was present with the other bishops in attendance. When he saw the philosopher insulting our people and proudly displaying his skill in dialectic, he asked everyone for a chance to exchange a few words with the philosopher. But our people, who knew only the man's simplicity and lack of skill in speech, feared that they might be put to shame in case his holy simplicity became a source of laughter to the clever. But the elder insisted, and he began his discourse in this way: "In the name of Jesus Christ, O philosopher," he said, "listen to the truth. There is one God who made heaven and earth, who gave breath to man whom he had formed from the mud of the earth, and who created everything, what is seen and what is not seen, with the power of his word and established it with the sanctification of his spirit. This word and wisdom, whom we call 'Son,' took pity on the errors of humankind, was born of a virgin, by suffering death freed us from everlasting death, and by his resurrection conferred on us eternal life. Him we await as the judge to come of all that we do. Do you believe that this is so, O philosopher?" But he, as though he had nothing whatever that he could say in opposition to this, so astonished was he at the power of what had been said, could only reply to it all that he thought that it was so, and that what had been said was the only truth. Then the elder said, "If you believe that this is so, arise, follow me to the church, and receive the seal of this faith." The philosopher, turning to his disciples and to those who had gathered to listen, said, "Listen, O learned men: so long as it was words with which I had to deal, I set words against words and what was said I refuted with my rhetoric. But when power rather than words came out of the mouth of the speaker, words could not withstand power, nor could man oppose God. And therefore if any one of you was able to feel in what was said what I felt, let him believe in Christ and follow this old man in whom God has spoken." And thus the philosopher became a Christian and rejoiced at last to have been vanquished.[5]

**10.4.** There was also at the council the man of God Bishop Paphnutius from Egypt, one of the confessors whom Maximian, after gouging out their right eyes and severing their left hams, had condemned to the mines. But there was in him such a grace of miracles that signs were worked through him no less than through the apostles of old. For he put demons to flight with a mere word and cured the sick by prayer alone. He is also said to have returned sight to the blind and given back soundness of body to the crippled. Constantine regarded him with such veneration and love that many times he called him into the palace, embraced him, and bestowed fervent kisses on the eye which had been gouged out in his confession of faith.[6]

**10.5.** If any of their number would have been even more outstanding, it is said to have been Spyridon, a bishop from Cyprus, a man belonging to the order of prophets, so much have we learned from what was said by those who saw him. He remained a shepherd even after he was appointed bishop. Now one night when thieves approached the fence and stretched forth their wicked hands to make an opening to bring out the sheep, they were held fast by invisible bonds and remained so until daybreak as though they had been handed over to torturers. But when the elder got ready to lead the sheep out to pasture in the morning, he saw the youths hanging stretched upon the fence without human bonds. When he had learned the reason for their punishment, he loosed with a word those whom he had deservedly bound, and lest they should have nothing to show for their nocturnal labors, he said, "Take one of the rams for yourselves, lads, so that you will not have come for nothing; but you would have done better to get it by request than by theft."[7]

They also relate of him the following miracle. He had a daughter named Irene who after she had faithfully served him died a virgin. After her death someone came who said he had entrusted to her a deposit. The father did not know of the affair. A search of the whole house failed to reveal anywhere what was sought. But the one who had left the deposit pressed his claim with weeping and tears, even avowing that he would take his own life if he could not recover what he had deposited. Moved by his tears, the old man hurried to his daughter's grave and called her by name. She said from the grave, "What do you want, father?" He replied, "Where did you put this man's deposit?" She explained where it was, saying, "You will find it buried there." Returning to the house, he found the thing where his daughter, from the grave, had said it was, and returned it to the one who had asked for it. There are many other miracles of his mentioned which are still talked about by all.[8]

There were, then, in those times as well very many shining examples of such men in the Lord's churches, of whom quite a few were present at the council. Athanasius, at that time a deacon of Alexander of Alexandria, was there too, aiding the old man with his assiduous advice. During that time the council met each day, and it did not dare to proceed carelessly or recklessly to a decision about such a serious matter. Arius was often summoned to the council, his propositions were discussed in painstaking detail, and the most careful consideration was given to the question of what position or decision to take against them. Finally after long and detailed discussion it was decided by all, and decreed as though by the mouth and heart of all, that the word *homoousios* should be written, that is that the Son should be acknowledged to be of the same substance as the Father, and this was most firmly declared by the vote of them all. There were then only seventeen, it is said, who preferred Arius's creed and who affirmed that God's Son had been created externally from nothing existing, and had not been begotten from the Father's very divinity. The decision of the council of priests was conveyed to Constantine, who revered it as though it had been pronounced by God and declared that anyone who should try to oppose it he would banish as transgressing divine decrees. Six only there were who suffered themselves to be expelled with Arius, while the other eleven, after taking counsel together, agreed to subscribe with hand only, not heart.[9] The chief designer of this pretence was Eusebius, bishop of Nicomedia. During that time, then, the subscriptions were written in whatever way, some sincerely and some not, as later events proved, particular regulations were made concerning each of several church customs, and so the council dissolved. There is here inserted a copy of the exposition of faith of those who had assembled.

## 10.6. Creed of Nicaea

"We believe in one God, the Father almighty, maker of all things visible and invisible, and in one Lord Jesus Christ, Son of God born as only-begotten of the Father, that is of the Father's substance, God from God, light from light, true God from true God, born not made, homoousios with the Father, that is of the same substance as the Father, through whom all things were made, those in heaven and those on earth. Who for the sake of us human beings and our salvation came down and was incarnate, and becoming a human being suffered and rose on the third day, and ascended to heaven, from where he is to come to judge the living and the dead. And in the Holy Spirit. But those who say that there was a time when he was not, and before he was born he was not, and that he was made out of nothing existing or who say that God's Son is from another subsistence or substance[10] or is subject to alteration or change, the catholic and apostolic church anathematizes.

I. They decree in addition[11] that it is to be observed in the churches that no one who castrates himself because of unwillingness to endure sexual desire is to be admitted to the clergy.

II. No one recently admitted to baptism from paganism and its way of life is to be made a cleric before being carefully examined.

III. No bishop or other cleric is to live with women who are not relatives, but only with his mother, sister, aunt, or persons related in this way.

IV. A bishop is if possible to be ordained by the bishops of the whole province. If this is difficult, then certainly by not fewer than three, but in such a way that either the presence or the authority of the metropolitan bishop in particular is involved. Without him they consider the ordination invalid.

V. A bishop is not to receive anyone, whether a cleric or a layman, whom another bishop has expelled from the church. Lest however there be no remedy for something which has been unjustly done because of some quarrel or bad temper, as sometimes happens, they decree that twice each year councils are to be held in each province by all the provincial bishops and judgment passed on such matters, so that if by chance something was done unjustly by one of them, it may be put right by the others, or if rightly, it may be confirmed by all.

VI. The ancient custom in Alexandria and the city of Rome is to be maintained whereby [the bishop of the former] has charge of Egypt, while [the bishop of the latter] has charge of the suburbicarian churches.[12]

VII. If by chance in ordaining a bishop two or three should disagree for some reason, the authority of the rest of them, and especially that of the metropolitan with the rest, is to be considered more valid.

VIII. The prerogative of honor given of old to the bishop of Jerusalem is to be preserved, the dignity of the metropolitan of that province being maintained nonetheless.

IX. As for the Cathari, whom we know as Novatianists, if they should repent and return to the church, having confessed the doctrines of the church: the clerics should be received into the clergy, but only after receiving ordination. Of course if one of their bishops comes to one of our bishops, he should sit in the place of the presbyters, but the title of bishop should remain with him alone who has ever held the Catholic faith, unless he has freely decided to honor him with that title, or if he has decided to look for a vacant bishopric for him. That is up to him.

X. There are not to be two bishops in one city.

XI. Those who are incautiously advanced to the priesthood and afterward confess some misdeed they have done, or are convicted by others, are to be deposed. Those also who are among the lapsed and who by chance have been ordained through ignorance are to be deposed when recognized.

XII. Those who although not tortured have lapsed during the persecutions and do penance sincerely are to spend five years among the catechumens and for two years after that are to be joined to the faithful in prayer alone, and in that way are afterward to be taken back.

XIII. Those who in order to confess the faith have left military service and then have once again sought to enter it are to do penance for thirteen years and afterward to be taken back, provided they do penance sincerely. It is also however in the bishop's power to adjust the term if he sees that they are giving careful and fruitful attention to their penance.

XIV. But as for those penitents who are dying, they decree that no time must be spent [doing penance]. If someone who has received communion recovers, however, he is to complete the times set or at least do as the bishop determines.

XV. As for catechumens who have lapsed, they have decreed that for three years they are to be separated from the prayer of the catechumens, and afterward to be taken back.

XVI. No one, whether a bishop or even another cleric, is to attempt to move from a lesser city to a greater church.

XVII. No cleric who for no good reason has left his church and roams about among the other churches is to be received into communion.

XVIII. No one is to steal away someone who belongs to someone else and ordain him a cleric in his own church without the consent of the one to whom he belongs.

XIX. No cleric is to charge interest, or an augmentation on grain or wine, the original amount of which when let out customarily yields a return of half again or even twice as much; if he does so, he is to be deposed as guilty of filthy lucre.

XX. Deacons are not to be given precedence over presbyters, nor are they to sit where the presbyters do or distribute the Eucharist when they are present; they are simply to assist while the others do that. But if there is no presbyter present, then only may they distribute as well; those that do otherwise are ordered to be deposed.

XXI. The Paulianists,[13] also called Photinians, are to be rebaptized.

XXII. Deaconesses likewise, because they do not in fact receive the imposition of hands, should also be placed among the laity."

So then once they had formulated decrees concerning these matters in a way consonant with respect for the divine laws, and also had handed down to the churches the ancient canon regarding the observance of Easter, so that no further inconsistency should arise, then everything was duly settled and the peace and faith of the churches was preserved, one and the same, in the East and the West.

10.7. It was at this time that Helena, Constantine's mother, a woman matchless in faith, devotion, and singular generosity, the sort of person whose son Constantine would be, and be considered to be, was alerted by divine visions and traveled to Jerusalem, where she asked the inhabitants where the place was where the sacred body of Christ had hung fastened to the gibbet. It was hard to find, because an image of Venus had been fixed there by the persecutors of old, so that if any Christian wished to worship Christ in that place, he would seem to be worshiping Venus. For this reason the place was unvisited and almost forgotten. But when, as we said, the pious woman had hastened to the place indicated to her by a sign from heaven, and had pulled away everything profane and defiled, she found deep down when the rubble had been cleared away three crosses jumbled together. But her joy at the discovery was darkened by the fact that the crosses were indistinguishable from each other. There was also found the inscription which Pilate had made with Greek, Latin, and Hebrew letters, but not even it showed clearly enough which was the Lord's gibbet. Here, then, human uncertainty demanded divine evidence.

There happened to be in the city a woman of high station who lived there and who was lying near death of a serious illness. Macarius was bishop of the church at the time. When he saw the perplexity of the empress and of all who were also present, he said, "Bring here all the crosses which have been found, and God will now disclose to us which one it was that bore God." And going in with the empress and the people to the woman who was lying there, he knelt down and poured out the following sort of prayer to God:

**10.8.** "O Lord, who through your only-begotten Son have deigned to bestow salvation on the human race through the suffering of the cross, and now have most recently inspired the heart of your handmaid to seek the blessed wood on which our salvation hung, show clearly which of these three was the cross destined for the Lord's glory, and which of them were made for servile punishment, that this woman who lies here half dead may be called back from the gates of death to life as soon as the healing wood touches her." Having said this, he first touched her with one of the three, but it did not help. He touched her with the second and again nothing happened. But when he touched her with the third, she at once opened her eyes, got up, and with renewed strength and far more liveliness than when she had been healthy before, she began to run about the whole house and glorify the Lord's power. The empress then, having been granted her prayer with such a clear token, poured her royal ambition into the construction of a wonderful temple on the site where she had found the cross. The nails too, with which the Lord's body had been fastened, she brought to her son. He made of some of them a bridle to use in battle, and with the others he is said to have equipped himself with a helmet no less useful in battle. As for the healing wood itself, part of it she presented to her son, and part she put in silver reliquaries and left in the place; it is still kept there as a memorial with unflagging devotion.[14]

The venerable empress also left the following mark of her religious spirit. She is said to have invited to lunch the virgins consecrated to God whom she found there and to have treated them with such devotion that she thought it unfitting for them to perform the duties of servants; rather, she herself, in servant's garb, set out the food with her own hands, offered the cup, and poured water over their hands, and the empress of the world and mother of the empire appointed herself servant of the servants of Christ.

This took place in Jerusalem. In the meantime Constantine, trusting in his faith, conquered by force of arms on their own soil the Sarmatians, the Goths, and the other barbarian nations,[15] except for those which had already achieved peace by treaties of friendship or self-surrender. The more he submitted to God in a spirit of religion and humility, the more widely God subjected everything to him. He also sent letters to Antony, the first desert-dweller, as to one of the prophets, begging him to beseech the Lord for him and his children.[16] Thus he longed to make himself acceptable to God not only by his own merits and his mother's devotion, but also through the intercession of the saints.

Now because we have mentioned the great man Antony, I would have liked to say something about his virtues, way of life, and soberness of mind, such that living alone he had only the companionship of wild animals, triumphed frequently over the demons, pleased God more than all other mortals, and left glorious examples of his way of life to the monks even of today, but the little book written by Athanasius and translated as well into Latin has forestalled me.[17] For this reason we will pass over what has already been said by others and mention those things which, however reliable the record of them may be, have escaped the notice of those far removed from them through not being so well known.

10.9. In the division of the earth which the apostles made by lot for the preaching of God's word, when the different provinces fell to one or the other of them, Parthia, it is said, went by lot to Thomas, to Matthew fell Ethiopia, and Hither India, which adjoins it, went to Bartholomew. Between this country and Parthia, but far inland, lies Further India. Inhabited by many peoples with many different languages, it is so distant that the plow of the apostolic preaching had made no furrow in it, but in Constantine's time it received the first seeds of faith in the following way. A philosopher named Metrodorus, they say, penetrated to Further India for the purpose of viewing the places and investigating the continent.[18] Encouraged by his example, a philosopher of Tyre named Meropius decided to go to India for the same reason; he had with him two small boys whom as his relatives he was instructing in letters. The younger was called Aedesius and the older Frumentius. When therefore the philosopher had seen fully and taken note of the things on which his mind was feasting, and he had set out on the return voyage, the ship in which he was sailing put in to some port to obtain water and other necessaries. It is the custom of the barbarians there that whenever the neighboring peoples announce that relations with the Romans have been disturbed, they kill all the Romans they find among them. The philosopher's ship was attacked and everyone with him put to death together. The boys, who were discovered under a tree going over and preparing their lessons, were saved because the barbarians pitied them and brought them to the king. He made one of them, Aedesius, his cupbearer, while to Frumentius, whose intelligence and prudence he could see, he entrusted his accounts and correspondence. From that time on they were held in high honor and affection by the king. Now when the king died and left as heir to the kingdom his wife and her young son, he also left it to the free choice of the youths what they would do. But the queen begged them to share with her the responsibility of ruling the kingdom until her son should grow up, as she had no one more trustworthy in the kingdom, especially Frumentius, whose prudence would suffice to rule the kingdom, for the other gave evidence simply of a pure faith and sober mind.

Now while they were doing so and Frumentius had the helm of the kingdom, God put it into his mind and heart to begin making careful inquiries if there were any Christians among the Roman merchants, and to give them extensive rights, which he urged them to use, to build places of assembly in each location, in which they might gather for prayer in the Roman manner. Not only that, but he himself did far more along these lines than anyone else, and in this way encouraged the others, invited them with his support and favors, made available whatever was suitable, furnished sites for buildings and everything else that was necessary, and bent every effort to see that the seed of Christians should grow up there.[19]

**10.10.** Now when the royal child whose kingdom they had looked after reached maturity, then, having executed their trust completely and handed it back faithfully, they returned to our continent, even though the queen and her son tried very hard to hold them back and asked them to stay. While Aedesius hastened to Tyre to see his parents and relatives again, Frumentius journeyed to Alexandria, saying that it was not right to conceal what the Lord had done. He therefore explained to the bishop everything that had been done and urged him to provide some worthy man to send as bishop to the already numerous Christians and churches built on barbarian soil. Then Athanasius, for he had recently received the priesthood,[20] after considering attentively and carefully what Frumentius had said and done, spoke as follows in the council of priests: "What other man can we find like you, in whom is God's spirit as in you, and who could achieve such things as these?" And having conferred on him the priesthood, he ordered him to return with the Lord's grace to the place from which he had come. When he had reached India as bishop, it is said that such a grace of miracles was given him by God that the signs of the apostles were worked by him and a countless number of barbarians was converted to the faith. From that time on there came into existence a Christian people and churches in India, and the priesthood began. These events we came to know of not from popular rumor, but from the report of Aedesius himself, who had been Frumentius's companion, and who later became a presbyter in Tyre.

**10.11.** It was at this time too that the Georgians, who dwell in the region of Pontus, accepted the word of God and faith in the kingdom to come. The cause of this great benefit was a woman captive who lived among them and led such a faithful, sober, and modest life, spending all of her days and nights in sleepless supplications to God, that the very novelty of it began to be wondered at by the barbarians. Their curiosity led them to ask what she was about. She replied with the truth: that in this manner she simply worshiped Christ as God. This answer made the barbarians wonder only at the novelty of the name, although it is true, as often happens, that her very perseverance made the common women wonder if she were deriving some benefit from such great devotion.

Now it is said that they have the custom that, if a child falls sick, it is taken around by its mother to each of the houses to see if anyone knows of a proven remedy to apply to the illness. And when one of the women had brought her child around to everyone, according to custom, and had found no remedy in any of the houses, she went to the woman captive as well to see if she knew of anything. She answered that she knew of no human remedy, but declared that Christ her God, whom she worshiped, could give it the healing despaired of by humans. And after she had put the child on her hair shirt and poured out above it her prayer to the Lord, she gave the infant back to its mother in good health. Word of this got around to many people, and news of the wonderful deed reached the ears of the queen, who was suffering from a bodily illness of the gravest sort and had been reduced to a state of absolute despair. She asked for the woman captive to be brought to her. She declined to go, lest she appear to pretend to more than was proper to her sex. The queen ordered that she herself be brought to the captive's hovel. Having placed her likewise on her hair shirt and invoked Christ's name, no sooner was her prayer done than she had her stand up healthy and vigorous, and taught her that it was Christ, God and Son of God most high, who had conferred healing upon her, and advised her to invoke him whom she should know to be the author of her life and well-being, for he it was who allotted kingdoms to kings and life to mortals. She returned joyfully home and disclosed the affair to her husband, who wanted to know the reason for this sudden return to health. When he in his joy at his wife's cure ordered gifts to be presented to the woman, she said, "O king, the captive deigns to accept none of these things. She despises gold, rejects silver, and battens on fasting as though it were food. This alone may we give her as a gift, if we worship as God the Christ who cured me when she called upon him."

But the king was not then inclined to do so and put it off for the time, although his wife urged him often, until it happened one day when he was hunting in the woods with his companions that a thick darkness fell upon the day, and with the light removed there was no longer any way for his blind steps through the grim and awful night. Each of his companions wandered off a different way, while he, left alone in the thick darkness which surrounded him, did not know what to do or where to turn, when suddenly there arose in his heart, which was near to losing hope of being saved, the thought that if the Christ preached to his wife by the woman captive were really God, he might now free him from this darkness so that he could from then on abandon all the others and worship him. No sooner had he vowed to do so, not even verbally but only mentally, than the daylight returned to the world and guided the king safely to the city. He explained directly to the queen what had happened. He required that the woman captive be summoned at once and hand on to him her manner of worship, insisting that from then on he would venerate no god but Christ. The captive came, instructed him that Christ is God, and explained, as far as it was lawful for a woman to disclose such things, the ways of making petition and offering reverence. She advised that a church be built and described its shape.

The king therefore called together all of his people and explained the matter from the beginning, what had happened to the queen and him, taught them the faith, and before even being initiated into sacred things became the apostle of his nation. The men believed because of the king, the women because of the queen, and with everyone desiring the same thing a church was put up without delay. The outer walls having quickly been raised, it was time to put the columns in place. When the first and second had been set up and they came to the third, they used all the machines and the strength of men and oxen to get it raised halfway up to an inclined position, but no machine could lift it the rest of the way, not even with efforts repeated again and again; with everyone exhausted, it would not budge. Everyone was confounded, the king's enthusiasm waned, and no one could think what to do. But when nightfall intervened and everyone went away and all mortal labors ceased, the woman captive remained inside alone, passing the night in prayer. And when the worried king entered in the morning with all his people, he saw the column, which so many machines and people had been unable to move, suspended upright just above its base: not placed upon it, but hanging about one foot in the air. Then indeed all the people looking on glorified God and accepted the witness of the miracle before them that the king's faith and the captive's religion were true. And behold, while everyone was still in the grip of wonder and astonishment, before their very eyes the column, with no one touching it, gradually and with perfect balance settled down upon its base. After that the remaining columns were raised with such ease that all that were left were put in place that day.

Now after the church had been magnificently built and the people were thirsting even more deeply for God's faith, on the advice of the captive an embassy of the entire people was sent to the emperor Constantine, and what had happened was explained to him. They implored him to send priests who could complete God's work begun among them. He dispatched them with all joy and honor, made far happier by this than if he had annexed to the Roman empire unknown peoples and kingdoms.[21] That this happened was related to us by that most faithful man Bacurius, the king of that nation who in our realm held the rank of *comes domesticorum* and whose chief concern was for religion and truth; when he was *dux limitis* in Palestine he spent some time with us in Jerusalem in great concord of spirit.[22] But let us return to our topic.

**10.12.** After Helena, the mother of the religious sovereign, had passed from this light laden with the highest honors of the Roman empire, Constantia, then Licinius's widow, was consoled by her brother, the Augustus. It happened that she came to be acquainted with a presbyter who covertly supported the Arian party. He at first divulged nothing at all of this to the sovereign's sister, but when long familiarity gave him his opportunity, he began gradually to suggest that Arius had been the target of envy, and that his bishop, stung by jealousy because Arius was so popular with the people, had stirred up the argument out of private motives of rivalry. By frequently saying these and the like things, he impressed his attitude upon Constantia. It is said that when she was dying and her brother was visiting her and speaking to her in a kindly and religious way, she asked him as a last favor to receive the presbyter into his friendship and to listen to whatever he would propose to him that had to do with his hope of salvation. She herself, she said, had no concerns now that she was departing from the light, but she was worried about her brother's situation, lest his empire fall to ruin on account of the innocent being punished. He accepted his sister's advice, believing that her concern for him was genuine, and lent his ear to the presbyter, in the meantime ordering Arius to be summoned from exile so that he could explain his views about the faith. Arius then composed a creed, which while it did not have the same meaning as ours, yet seemed to contain our words and profession. The emperor was indeed amazed, and thought that the very same views were set out in his exposition as in that of the council held previously. But in no respect did he slacken his vigilance of mind; he referred him once again to a council's scrutiny, for in fact priests from all over the world were being invited to gather for the dedication of Jerusalem. He wrote to them concerning him that if they approved his exposition of faith and found either that he had previously been convicted unjustly out of jealousy, as he maintained, or was now corrected of his error, they should judge him with clemency, if, that is, his bishop, Alexander, would agree; such after all had been the moderation of the council that it had passed sentence, not against his person, but against the falsehood of his doctrines. But those who from the first had supported his endeavors and subscribed insincerely made no difficulty about receiving him. When he reached Alexandria, however, he could get nowhere with his plans, because while tricks work with the ignorant, they just raise a laugh from the knowledgeable.[23]

In the meantime, while this vain commotion was going on in Alexandria, the venerable Augustus Constantine died in a suburban villa of Nicomedia in the thirty-first year of his reign, having left his children written in his will as heirs in succession to the Roman world. Because Constantius, to whom he had bequeathed the Eastern empire, was not present at the time, it is said that he summoned in secret the presbyter who we said earlier had been recommended by his sister and had thereafter been held in friendship, entrusted to him the will he had written, and bound him by oath to hand it over to no one but Constantius, when he came. Since the palace eunuchs were also on his side, news of the emperor's death was skillfully suppressed until Constantius's arrival, many who tried to seize power were put down, and the state remained safe and undamaged. But when Constantius arrived, the presbyter restored what had been committed to him. The emperor in his desire for the realm was on account of this favor so bound to him that, anxious as he was to govern others, he cheerfully allowed himself to be governed by him. From that time on, having subjugated the emperor to himself, he began to speak about restoring Arius and to urge him to compel the priests who were reluctant to agree.[24]

**10.13.** At that time the priesthood was being exercised in Alexandria by Alexander, in Jerusalem by Maximus the confessor, and in Constantinople likewise by Alexander, as we learn from the writings of Athanasius. Now Eusebius, who was in Nicomedia and about whose pretence in subscribing we spoke earlier, seized his chance: having become friendly with the sovereign through the offices of the presbyter, he bent his efforts to rolling everything back and rendering invalid the council's actions. He got Arius, who was residing in Alexandria to no purpose, to come, and through imperial edicts had a fresh council summoned to Constantinople. Those who convened were mostly of the party of Arius and Eusebius. Time and again they met with Alexander to try to get him to receive Arius, but they did not defeat him, however much abuse they poured on him. Finally they told him they were setting a day on which either he would receive Arius or, if he refused, he should realize that he would be driven from the church and into exile, and someone else would receive him. Alexander spent the whole night before the day in question lying at the foot of the altar in tears and prayer, commending the church's cause to the Lord. When dawn had broken and Alexander continued in prayer, Eusebius with all of his company, like the standard-bearer of an army of heretics, went up in the morning to Arius's house and bade him follow him to the church without delay, declaring that Alexander, unless he were present and consented, should be driven from the place.

**10.14.** Everyone therefore was waiting with great interest to see where the perseverance of Alexander or the importunity of Eusebius and Arius would lead; the importance of the affair was holding everyone in suspense. Arius, hemmed in by a crowd of bishops and laity, was making his way to the church when he turned aside at a call of nature to a public facility. And when he sat down, his intestines and all his innards slipped down into the privy drain, and thus it was in such a place that he met a death worthy of his foul and blasphemous mind. When news of this was later brought to the church to Eusebius and to those with him who were pressing the holy and innocent Alexander to receive Arius, they departed overcome with shame and covered with confusion. Then was fulfilled to the glory of the Lord the word which Alexander had cried out to God in prayer, saying, "Judge, O Lord, between me and the threats of Eusebius and the violence of Arius!" Now these events caused some slight and short-lived embarrassment; but the heretics met together, fearful that the affair would be reported to the emperor Constantius just as it happened, and that not only would he disown their perfidy, in which he had so cleverly been ensnared, but would also visit upon the authors of his deception stern treatment through his imperial power. They therefore arranged through the eunuchs, whom they had already won over to their perfidy, that, as far as could be done, the emperor should hear a commonly agreed-upon version of Arius's death, and that he should learn nothing that would hint of God's punishment. Having done this, they continued the efforts they had begun with respect to the faith.[25]

**10.15.** Athanasius, then, received the see of Alexandria upon the death of Alexander. Now the heretics were already well aware that he was a man of keen intelligence and altogether tireless in the management of the church, since he had come to the Council of Nicaea with his old bishop Alexander, by whose counsel the tricks and deceits of the heretics had been unremittingly exposed. As soon, then, as they found out that he had been made bishop, they concluded that their concerns would find no easy way past his vigilance, as in fact turned out to be true, and so they cast about everywhere for deceptions to use against him.

Now I do not think it out of place to trace back briefly his early years and to explain how he was educated as a boy, as we have found out from those who lived with him. Once when Bishop Alexander was celebrating the day of Peter Martyr in Alexandria, he was waiting in a place near the sea after the ceremonies were over for his clergy to gather for a banquet. There he saw from a distance some boys on the seashore playing a game in which, as they often do, they were mimicking a bishop and the things customarily done in church. Now when he had gazed intently for a while at the boys, he saw that they were also performing some of the more secret and sacramental things. He was disturbed and immediately ordered the clergy to be called to him and showed them what he was watching from a distance. Then he commanded them to go and get all the boys and bring them to him. When they arrived, he asked them what game they were playing and what they had done and how. At first they were afraid, as is usual at that age, and refused, but then they disclosed in due order what they had done, admitting that some catechumens had been baptized by them at the hands of Athanasius, who had played the part of bishop in their childish game. Then he carefully inquired of those who were said to have been baptized what they had been asked and what they had answered, and the same of him who had put the questions, and when he saw that everything was according to the manner of our religion, he conferred with a council of clerics and then ruled, so it is reported, that those on whom water had been poured after the questions had been asked and answered correctly need not repeat the baptism, but that those things should be completed which are customarily done by priests. As for Athanasius and those who had played the parts of presbyters and ministers in the game, he called together their parents, and having put them under oath, handed them over to be reared for the church. But a short time later, after Athanasius had been thoroughly educated by a scribe and received adequate instruction from a teacher of literature, he was at once given back to the priest by his parents, like a deposit from the Lord kept faithfully, and like another Samuel was brought up in the Lord's temple. And so he was appointed by Alexander, as he was going to his fathers in a good old age, to wear the priestly ephod after him.[26]

But he had such struggles to undergo in the church for the integrity of the faith that the following passage seems to have been written about him too: "I will show him how much he will have to suffer for my name."[27] For the whole world conspired to persecute him and the princes of the earth were moved,[28] nations, kingdoms, and armies gathered against him. But he guarded that divine utterance which runs: "If camps are set up against me, my heart will not fear, if battle is waged against me, in him will I hope."[29] But because his deeds are so outstanding that their greatness does not allow me to omit any of them, yet their number compels me to pass over very many, and thus my mind is troubled by uncertainty, unable to decide which to keep and which to pass over. We shall therefore relate a few of the pertinent matters, leaving the rest to be told by his fame, which will, however, doubtless find itself recounting the lesser things. For it will discover nothing that it could add.

**10.16.** When Constantius, then, had obtained sole control of the Eastern empire upon the death of his brother Constantine,[30] who was killed by soldiers not far from Aquileia by the river Alsa, Constans, the brother of them both, was ruling the West with fair diligence. Constantius, to be sure, was of royal nature and mind and carefully cultivated those mainstays of his rule, but he was cleverly deceived into supporting perfidy by depraved priests who used the eunuchs, and he eagerly supported their wicked designs. But they feared that Athanasius might sometime gain access to the sovereign and teach him, according to the scriptures, the truth about the faith, which they were distorting. So they proceeded to accuse him to the sovereign in every possible way of every sort of crime and outrage, even to the point of showing the emperor an arm from a human body which they presented in a case, claiming that Athanasius had severed it from the body of one Arsenius in order to use it for magic. They made up as well a great many other crimes and misdeeds.

**10.17.** Their purpose was that the emperor might order Athanasius to be condemned at a council he would summon, and he did order one to convene at Tyre, sending as his representative one of the counts. He was assisted by Archelaus, then Count of Oriens, and by the governor of the province of Phoenicia. There Athanasius was brought, the case with the human arm was shown around, and an indignant horror invaded the souls of all, religious and ordinary folk alike.

**10.18.** This Arsenius, whose arm was supposed to have been cut off, had once been a lector of Athanasius, but fearing rebuke for some fault, he had withdrawn from his company. These outrageous men considered his concealment ideal for their schemes, and kept him hidden, when they began to hatch their plot, with someone they believed they could fully trust with their misdeed. But while in hiding he heard of the crime they intended to commit in his name against Athanasius. Moved either by human feeling or by divine providence, he secretly escaped his confinement in the silence of the night, sailed to Tyre, presented himself to Athanasius on the day before the final day for pleading his case, and explained the affair from the beginning. Athanasius ordered him to stay in the house and not let anyone know he was there. In the meantime the council was summoned; some of those who gathered were aware of the calumny concocted, and almost everyone was hostile to and prejudiced against Athanasius. The confessor Paphnutius, whom we mentioned earlier, was there at the time and was aware of Athanasius's innocence. Now he saw Bishop Maximus of Jerusalem sitting with the others whom the shameful plot had united; together with him he had had an eye gouged out and a ham severed and thus become a confessor, but because of his excessive simplicity he suspected nothing of the monstrous behavior of the priests. He went up to him fearlessly where he was sitting in their midst and said, "Maximus, you bear along with me one and the same mark of confession, and for you as much as for me the gouging out of the mortal eye has procured the brighter sight of the divine light. I will not let you sit in the council of evildoers and go in with the workers of malice." And taking hold of him he lifted him up from their midst, informed him in detail of what was taking place, and joined him thereafter in lasting communion to Athanasius.

In the meantime the case was being presented. First to be introduced was the charge of some woman who said that she had once received Athanasius as a guest and during the night, suspecting nothing, had been forcibly violated by him. Athanasius was ordered to be presented to her. He entered with his presbyter Timothy and told him that after the woman had finished speaking, he himself would keep still and Timothy should respond to what she had said. So when the woman had finished the speech she had been taught, Timothy turned to her and said, "Is it true, woman, that I once stayed with you? Or that I forced you, as you claim?" Then she, with the effrontery common to such women, leaned toward Timothy and said, "You, you forced me; you defiled my chastity in that place." At the same time, turning to the judges, she began to swear to God that she was telling the truth. Then embarrassment at being made ridiculous began to come over everyone, because the plot involving the crime which had been invented had so easily been laid bare without the accused having said anything. But the judges were not allowed to question the woman about where she was from or by whom and how the calumny had been devised, since liberty of judgment rested with the accusers. They proceeded from this to the other charge. A crime was revealed never before heard of. "Here," they said, "we have something about which no one can be deceived by artful speech; the matter is something for the eyes, and speech falls silent. This severed arm accuses you, Athanasius. This is Arsenius's right arm; explain how you cut it off or to what purpose." He replied, "Which of you knew Arsenius and may recognize that this is his right arm?" Some of them stood up and said that they knew Arsenius quite well; among them were several who had no knowledge of the plot. Athanasius then asked the judges to order his man brought in whom the matter required. When Arsenius had been brought in, Athanasius lifted his face and said to the council and the judges, "This is Arsenius." And raising his right hand likewise, he said, "This is also his right hand and this his left. But as for where this hand comes from which they have presented, that is for you to investigate." Then something like night and darkness fell upon the eyes of the accusers, who did not know what to do or where to turn. For the witnesses confirmed that it was Arsenius, whom they had just before said they knew. But because the council was being held not to judge but to put down the man, a clamor suddenly arose from all sides that Athanasius was a sorcerer who was deceiving the eyes of the onlookers, and that such a man should by no means be allowed to live any longer. And they rushed at him, ready to tear him apart with their hands. But Archelaus, who with the others was presiding at the council by the emperor's command, snatched him from the hands of his assailants, led him out by secret ways, and advised him to seek safety by flight, as it was the only way he could reach it. The council however met again as though nothing whatever had come to light and condemned Athanasius as having confessed to the crimes with which he had been charged. And having concocted minutes in this form and sent them throughout the world, they forced the other bishops to assent to their crime, the emperor compelling them to this.[31]

**10.19.** Hence Athanasius was now a fugitive at large in the whole world, and there remained for him no safe place to hide. Tribunes, governors, counts, and even armies were deployed by imperial orders to hunt him down. Rewards were offered to informers to bring him in alive if possible, or at least his head. Thus the whole power of the empire was directed in vain against the man with whom God was. During this time he is said to have remained concealed for six successive years in a dry cistern, never seeing the sun. But when his presence was revealed by a servant woman, who seems to have been the only one aware of the good offices of her masters who offered him concealment, then as though warned by God's Spirit, he moved to another place on the very night they came with informers to arrest him, six years after having come there. Those therefore who had come in vain, and who found that the owners too had fled, punished the servant woman as a false informer.

**10.20.** But lest his concealment cause trouble for someone and provide an opportunity for calumniating the innocent, the fugitive, presuming that there was no safe place for him any longer in Constantius's realm, withdrew to Constans's region. He was received by him honorably and in a religious spirit. And having carefully investigated his case, news of which had reached him, he wrote to his brother that he had learned as something certain that the priest of God most high Athanasius had undergone flight and exile unjustly. He would therefore do the right thing if he restored him to his place without causing him any trouble; if he did not want to do so, then he would take care of the matter himself by making his way to the innermost part of his realm and subjecting the authors of the crime to the punishment they richly deserved. Constantius, terrified by the letter because he realized that his brother was capable of carrying out his threat, bade Athanasius with pretended kindness to come to him of his own accord, and, having rebuked him lightly, allowed him to proceed to his own church in safety. The emperor, though, at the prompting of his impious counselors said, "The bishops have a small favor to ask of you, Athanasius: that you concede one of the many churches in Alexandria to the people who do not wish to hold communion with you." But at God's prompting he found a stratagem on the spot. "O emperor," he replied, "Is there anything that may be denied you if you request it, seeing that you have the power to command everything? But there is one thing I ask: that you allow me also a small request." He promised to grant anything he wanted, even if it was difficult, if only he would concede this one thing, so Athanasius said, "What I ask is that since there are some people of ours here as well"—for this interview was taking place in Antioch—"and they do not want to communicate with them, one church may be given over to their use." The emperor happily promised this, since it seemed to him quite just and easy to grant. When he presented the matter to his counselors, however, they answered that they wished neither to accept a church there nor to yield one in their city, since each of them was looking to his own interests rather than to those of people not present. The emperor, then, marveling at his prudence, bade him hurry off to receive his church.[32]

But when Magnentius's villainy had robbed the emperor Constans of his life and his realm together, then once again those who in past times had incited the sovereign against Athanasius began to revive his hatred, and when he had fled from the church they sent in his place George, their companion in perfidy and cruelty. For first they had sent Gregory. Once again there was flight and concealment, and imperial edicts against Athanasius were put up everywhere promising rewards and honors to informants. The sovereign too, when he had come into the West to avenge his brother's murder and recover his realm, and had taken sole possession of the empire once the usurper was eliminated, proceeded to wear out the Western bishops and by deception to compel them to assent to the Arian heresy; to this the condemnation of Athanasius was prefixed, he being as it were the great barrier which had first to be removed.

**10.21.** For this reason a council of bishops was summoned to Milan. Most of them were taken in, but Dionysius, Eusebius, Paulinus, Rhodanius, and Lucifer announced that there was treachery lurking in the proceedings, asserting that the subscription against Athanasius had no other end in view than the destruction of the faith. They were driven into exile. Hilary joined them too, the others either not knowing of the trick or not believing that there was one.[33]

**10.22.** But subsequent events showed that such had been the plan behind the proceeding. For once they had been gotten out of the way, no time was lost in summoning a synod to Ariminum. There shrewd and cunning men easily tricked the simple and inexperienced Western priests in a manner consistent with what the Easterners had fashioned at Seleucia, putting the question to them in this way: Whom do you prefer to adore and worship, the *homoousios* or Christ? But since they did not know what the word *homoousios* meant, such talk aroused disgust and abhorrence in them, and they declared that they believed in Christ, not the *homoousios*. Thus the majority, with the exception of a few who knowingly lapsed, were deceived, and set themselves against what the fathers at Nicaea had written, decreeing that *homoousios* should be removed from the creed as a word unknown and foreign to scripture, and defiling their communion by associating with the heretics. This was the time when the face of the church was foul and exceedingly loathsome, for now it was ravaged, not as previously by outsiders, but by its own people. Those banished and those who banished them were all members of the church. Nowhere was there altar, immolation, or libation, but there was nonetheless transgression, lapse, and the ruin of many. Alike was the punishment, unequal the victory. Alike was the affliction, unequal the boast, for the church grieved over the fall of those as well who forced the others to lapse.[34]

**10.23.** Liberius, then, was exercising the priesthood at the time in the city of Rome following Julius, the successor of Mark, whom Silvester had preceded; he was banished, and his deacon Felix was put in his place by the heretics. Felix was tainted not so much by sectarian difference as by the connivance surrounding his communion and ordination.[35]

**10.24.** In Jerusalem Cyril now received the priesthood after Maximus in an irregular ordination, and wavered sometimes in doctrine and often in communion. In Alexandria George exercised the episcopacy seized by force with such lack of moderation that he seemed to think he had been entrusted with a magistracy and not a priesthood involving religious duties.[36]

**10.25.** In Antioch a great many things were certainly done in a decidedly irregular fashion at various times. For after the death of Eudoxius, when many bishops from various cities were doing their utmost to acquire the see, they finally transferred there Meletius of Sebaste, a city in Armenia, contrary to the decrees of the council. But they drove him back into exile, because against their expectation he began to preach in church not Arius's faith, but ours. A large group of people who followed him when he was ejected from the church was sundered from the heretics' fellowship.[37]

**10.26.** In the meantime, that the luxuriant evil might at last turn its rage on its own self too, the priests and people who under Arius's guidance had been originally sundered from the church were split afresh into three sects and parties. Those who we earlier said had not agreed to the pretenses of Eusebius and the rest, but had suffered exile with Arius, would not even hold communion afterward with Arius himself when he returned from exile, because with his feigned confession he had accepted communion with those who acknowledged that the Son is of the same substance as the Father. With quite unrestrained or rather impudent blasphemy they maintained what Arius had first taught: that the Son had not been born but created and made out of what did not exist. After their death one Aetius propounded this, and after Aetius Eunomius developed the doctrine even more vigorously and extensively. He was a man leprous in body and soul and outwardly afflicted with jaundice, but exceedingly able in debate; he wrote much against our faith and gave principles of disputation to the members of his sect. Even today the Eunomian heresy is named after him. There was another named Macedonius, whom after ejecting or rather killing our people in Constantinople they had ordained bishop and whom because he acknowledged the Son as like the Father they ejected, even though he blasphemed the Holy Spirit just as they did. The reason was that he was teaching concerning the Son things similar to what he said of the Father. But he is not associated with our people, his views about the Spirit being at variance with ours. Thus that fell beast, which Arius had first caused to raise its head as though from the underworld, suddenly appeared in triple form: the Eunomians, who say that the Son is in all respects different from the Father, because in no way can what is made be like its maker; the Arians, who say that the Son can indeed be said to be like the Father, but by the gift of grace, not by a natural property, to the extent, that is, that a creature may be compared to the Creator; and the Macedonians, who say that while the Son is in all respects like the Father, the Holy Spirit has nothing in common with the Father and the Son. This is what took place among them, but as is written of such people: "They were torn but not stung to repentance."[38] For very many of those who apparently led a strict life, and a great number of monasteries in Constantinople and the neighboring provinces, and noble bishops, followed rather Macedonius's error.

**10.27.** But the emperor Constantius, while he was preparing to go with an army against Julian, whom he had left as Caesar in Gaul and who had on his own presumed to take the rank of Augustus, died at Mopsucrenae, a town in Cilicia, in the twenty-fourth year of his reign after his father's death.[39]

**10.28.** After him Julian as sole ruler received as a legitimate sovereignty what he had presumed to take. At first, as though critical of what Constantius had done, he bade the bishops be released from exile, but afterward he rose against our people with every hurtful stratagem. At that time the bishops still left there were released from exile. For Liberius, bishop of the city of Rome, had returned while Constantius was still alive; but whether this was because he had agreed voluntarily to subscribe, or whether it was a favor to the Roman people, who had interceded for him as he was going forth, I have not discovered for certain.

Now Eusebius begged Lucifer, since they had both been exiled to neighboring parts of Egypt, to go with him to Alexandria to see Athanasius and together with the priests still there to formulate a common policy regarding the situation of the church. But he refused to attend, sending instead his deacon to represent him, and with set purpose made his way to Antioch. There the parties were still at odds, but hopeful of reunion if the sort of bishop could be chosen for them with whom not just one people but both could be satisfied; but Lucifer with excessive haste ordained as bishop Paulinus, a man certainly Catholic, holy, and in all respects worthy of the priesthood, but not someone to whom both peoples could agree.[40]

**10.29.** Eusebius meanwhile made his way to Alexandria, where a council of confessors gathered, few in number but pure in faith and numerous in merits, to discuss with all care and deliberation in what way tranquillity might be restored to the church after the storms of heresy and disturbances of perfidy. Some fervent spirits thought that no one should be taken back into the priesthood who had in any way stained himself by communion with the heretics. But others in imitation of the apostle sought not what was advantageous to themselves but to the many, and followed the example of Christ who, being the life of all, humbled himself for the salvation of all and went down to his death, that in this way life might be found even among the dead; they said that it was better to humble themselves a little for the sake of those cast down, and bend a little for the sake of those crushed, that they might raise them up again and not keep the kingdom of heaven for themselves alone on account of their purity. It would be more glorious if they merited to enter there with many others, and therefore they thought the right thing was to get rid of the authors of the perfidy alone, giving the other priests the option, if they wished, of renouncing the error of perfidy and returning to the faith of the fathers. Nor should they deny admission to those returning, but should rather rejoice at their return, because the younger son in the gospel too, who had wasted his father's property, merited not only to be taken back when he had come to his senses, but was regarded as worthy of his father's embraces and received the ring of faith and had the robe put on him; and what did the robe signify but the tokens of priesthood? The older son did not win his father's approval by his jealousy of the one who was taken back, nor did the merit he had gained by not misbehaving equal the censure he incurred by not showing leniency to his brother.[41]

**10.30.** When therefore that priestly and apostolic body had approved these counsels brought forth from the gospel, responsibility for the East was, by decree of the council, committed to Asterius and to the others with them, while the West was assigned to Eusebius. There was of course included in the conciliar decree a fuller treatment of the Holy Spirit as well: that the Holy Spirit too should be believed to be of the same substance and divinity as the Father and Son, and there should be no mention at all of anything created or inferior or posterior in the

Trinity. There was also a discussion about the difference between "substances" and "subsistences" in relation to scripture; in Greek these terms are *ousiai* and *hypostaseis*. Some said that they thought that "substance" and "subsistence" meant the same thing, and as we do not speak of three substances in God, neither should we speak of three subsistences. Others, however, who thought that "substance" meant something very different than "subsistence," said that "substance" designated simply the nature of a thing and its inner constitution, whereas "subsistence" indicated the fact of the existence of each person as a subsistent entity. For this reason, because of the heresy of Sabellius, three subsistences should be confessed, since that would make it clear that three subsistent persons were meant and eliminate any suspicion that we belong to that faith which acknowledges the Trinity only nominally and not in essential reality. There was also included a statement about the incarnation of the Lord, that the body which the Lord assumed lacked neither the faculty of perception nor a soul. All of which having been stated with balance and moderation, each went his own way in peace.[42]

**10.31.** But Eusebius, when he had returned to Antioch and found there a bishop ordained by Lucifer contrary to his promise, left in shame and indignation without granting his communion to either party, because upon his departure from there he had promised to see to it in the council that that person would be ordained bishop from whom neither party would defect. For the people who had remained loyal to Meletius on account of his orthodoxy after he had been driven from the church had not joined the earlier Catholics, those, that is, who had been with Bishop Eustathius and among whom was Paulinus, but maintained their own autonomy and place of assembly. Eusebius wanted to reunite these people, but since he had been forestalled by Lucifer, he could not, and so he departed. Then when Meletius returned from exile, since the people with him was more numerous, he took over the churches and from then on maintained his own alliance with other Eastern bishops,[43] and he was not joined with Athanasius.

Meanwhile Lucifer, taking it hard that Eusebius had not accepted the bishop he had ordained in Antioch, thought that he in turn might not accept the decisions of the Council of Alexandria, but he was constrained by the bond of his representative, who had subscribed at the council with his authority. For he could not reject him who possessed his authority; but if he received him, he had to watch all his plans go for nought. Having thought long and hard about this, since there was no way out he decided to receive his legate and to preserve a different judgment about the others, one that was more satisfactory to him. He returned therefore to Sardinia, and I am not sure whether his death arrived too soon for him to change his mind—for rash initiatives are usually corrected by time—or whether he maintained his attitude unwaveringly. In any event, it is from here that the Luciferian schism, which still has a few adherents, took its start. Eusebius for his part went around the East and Italy acting as physician and priest alike. He recalled the churches, one by one, to the renunciation of infidelity and soundness of orthodoxy, especially when he discovered that Hilary, who we mentioned earlier had been banished with the other bishops, had already returned and from his place of residence in Italy was making the same efforts to restore the churches and revive the faith of the fathers.

**10.32.** The only difference was that Hilary, a man naturally gentle and peaceful and at the same time learned and most adept at persuasion, was achieving his purpose more carefully and skillfully. He also published some excellent books about the faith, in which he so carefully expounded both the cunning of the heretics and the way in which our people had been deceived and their unfortunate gullibility, that with his faultless teaching he corrected both those with him and those far off whom he could not address in person. Thus these two men, like two great lights of the world, lit up Illyricum, Italy, and Gaul with their brightness, so that all the darkness of heresy was driven from even the most remote and hidden corners.[44]

**10.33.** Now Julian, once he had come into the East to drive out the Persians by war and began to be carried away by an unconcealed craze for idolatry which earlier he had kept secret, showed himself more astute than the others as a persecutor in that he ruined almost more people by rewards, honors, flattery, and persuasion, than if he had proceeded by way of force, cruelty, and torture. Forbidding Christians access to the study of pagan authors, he decreed that elementary schools should be open only to those who worshiped the gods and goddesses. He ordered that posts in the armed and civil services should be given only to those who sacrificed. He decreed that the government of provinces and the administration of justice should not be entrusted to Christians, since their own law forbade them to use the sword. And he progressed daily in seeking out such laws as embodied all sorts of ingenious and cunning policies, although they did not appear particularly cruel.

**10.34.** But he could not keep up the pretence of philanthropy toward Athanasius. For when like horrid serpents bursting forth from their lairs his impious band of sorcerers, philosophers, diviners, and soothsayers had made its way to him, they all alike declared that they would accomplish nothing by their arts unless he first got rid of Athanasius, the one who stood in the way of them all.

**10.35.** Once again an army was sent, once again officers, again the church was assaulted. And when the people stood around him in grief and tears, he is said to have spoken to them prophetically. "Do not," he said, "be distressed, my children, because this is a small cloud which passes quickly." And when he had left and was making his way by boat on the Nile River, the count who had been sent for this purpose found out which way he had gone and set out after him without delay. And when by chance Athanasius's boat had put in at a certain place, he learned from the passers-by that his assassin was behind him and that at any moment, if he did not look out, he would be upon him. All those with him were terrified and tried to persuade him to seek refuge in the desert. But he said, "Do not be frightened, my children; let us rather go to meet our executioner, that he may realize that the one protecting us is far greater than the one pursuing us." And turning his boat around he set his course to meet his pursuer. He in turn, having no reason to suspect that the one he was after was coming toward him, ordered the company to be asked, as though they were passers-by, if they had heard where Athanasius was. When they replied that they had seen him on the move not far off, he hurried by with all speed, hastening in vain to capture the man he could not see before his very eyes. But he, guarded by God's strength, returned to Alexandria and there remained safely in hiding until the persecution ceased.[45]

**10.36.** Julian also gave another sign of his madness and folly. When he had offered sacrifice to Apollo by the Castalian spring in Daphne, a suburb of Antioch, but had received no answers to his questions and asked the priests of the demon the reasons for the silence, they said, "The burial place of the martyr Babylas is nearby and for that reason no answers are given." Then he ordered the Galileans, for thus he called our people, to come and remove the martyr's tomb. The whole church therefore came together, mothers and husbands, virgins and youths, and with immense rejoicing pulled along the martyr's coffin in a long procession singing psalms with loud cries and exultation and saying, "May all those be put to shame who worship carven idols and who trust in their images." This psalm the whole church sang in the hearing of the sacrilegious sovereign over a distance of six miles with such exultation that the sky rang with the shouts. He became so furious that the next day he ordered Christians to be arrested at random, thrust into prison, and subjected to punishment and torture.

**10.37.** Salutius, his prefect, did not approve of this, although he was a pagan, but he followed his order and tortured a youth named Theodore, the first who chanced to be arrested, from first light until the tenth hour with such cruelty and so many changes of torturers that history cannot recall the like. Raised aloft on the rack and with a torturer busy on either side of him, he did nothing but repeat with a calm and joyous countenance the psalm which the whole church had sung the day before. When Salutius saw that he had exhausted all his cruelty to no purpose, he is said to have returned the youth to prison, gone to the emperor, reported what he had done, and advised him not to try anything else of the sort, or else he would win glory for them and ignominy for himself. We ourselves later saw Theodore in Antioch, and when we asked him if he had felt the pain fully, he said that while he had felt some slight pain, a youth had stood by him wiping away his perspiration with the purest white cloth while he was sweating and had kept applying cool water to him, and he had enjoyed it so much that he was unhappy when he was ordered off the rack. The emperor, then, threatening to do a better job of subduing the Christians after his victory over the Persians, set out but never returned. Wounded either by his own men or by the enemy, we do not know which, he brought to an end there his reign as Augustus, upon which he had presumed to enter, after a year and eight months.[46]

**10.38.** Now such was his refined cunning in deception that he even deluded the unhappy Jews, enticing them with the sort of vain hopes that he himself entertained. First of all, summoning them to him he asked them why they did not sacrifice, when their law included commandments for them about sacrifices. Thinking an opportunity had come their way, they answered, "We cannot do so except in the temple in Jerusalem. For thus the law ordains." And having received from him permission to repair the temple, they grew so arrogant that it was as though some prophet had come back to them. Jews came together from every place and province and began to make their way to the site of the temple, long since consumed by fire, a count having been assigned by the emperor to push forward the work, which was pursued with all earnestness and financed both publicly and privately. Meanwhile they insulted our people and as though the time of the kingdom had returned threatened them harshly and treated them cruelly; in a word, they behaved with monstrous arrogance and pride. Cyril was the bishop of Jerusalem, following Maximus the confessor. The foundations, then, having been cleared, and quicklime and stone procured, nothing more was needed before new foundations could be laid the next day once the old ones had been dislodged. The bishop, however, having carefully weighed what was contained in Daniel's prophecy about the times on the one hand, and what the Lord had foretold in the gospels on the other, insisted that the Jews would never be able to put a stone upon a stone there. Thus the suspense grew.[47]

**10.39.** And behold, on the night which alone remained before the work was to begin, there was a violent earthquake, and not only were the stones for the foundations tossed far and wide, but almost all the buildings round about were leveled to the ground. The public porticoes too, in which the multitude of Jews was staying who were working on the project, tumbled to the ground, burying all the Jews inside.

At daybreak, thinking it had escaped the misfortune, the remaining multitude hurried together to look for those who had been buried.

**10.40.** Now there was a chamber sunk down in the interior of the temple which had its entrance between two porticoes that had been leveled to the ground; in it were kept some iron implements and other things necessary for the work. Out of it there suddenly burst a globe of fire which sped through the square, weaving this way and that and burning and killing the Jews who were there. This happened again and again with great frequency throughout the whole day, checking the rashness of the obstinate people with the avenging flames, while meantime all who were there were in such great fear and trembling that they were forced, however unwillingly, to abandon their plans and admit that Jesus Christ is the one true God. And so that these things would not be held to have happened by chance, on the following night the sign of the cross appeared on everyone's clothing so clearly that even those who in their unbelief wanted to wash it off could find no way to get rid of it. Thus the Jews and the pagans in their fright abandoned both the site and the useless project.[48]

### NOTES TO BOOK 10

1. *Sacerdos* and *sacerdotium* are as usual translated as "priest" and "priesthood" throughout. The reader should be aware, however, that in the Christian Latin of the period the words, when referring to the Christian clergy, normally mean "bishop" and "episcopacy."

2. On the succession of Peter (300–311), Achillas (311–312), and Alexander (313–328), cf. Theodoret 1.2.8. On Arius's religious appearance, cf. Epiphan. *Pan.* 69.3.1. On Arius's teaching, cf. Hanson 3–18; C. Stead, "Arius in Modern Research," *JTS*, N.S., 45 (1994), 24–36.

On the break between Alexander and Arius, cf. Epiphan. *Pan.* 68.4.1–3 and 69.3–9; Theodoret 1.2.12; *Philostorgius*, 1.7ᵃ.

On the Council of Nicaea, cf. Eusebius *VC* 3.6–21; Athan. *De decretis* 19–20, *Ad Afros* 5; Soc. 1.8; Opitz *Urk.* 20–26; Hefele-Leclercq 1.423–449; *Histoire des conciles oecuméniques*, vol. 1: I. Ortiz de Urbina, *Nicée et Constantinople* (Paris, 1963), 15–136; Hanson 152–178. The number of 318 bishops attending the council became traditional, but the actual number seems to have been lower, and it fluctuated during the summer. Perhaps there were around 250 there: cf. R. Williams, *Arius* (London, 1987), 67.

3. Ps. 82:1; Soc. 1.8.18–20; Soz. 1.17.3–6.

4. 1 Cor. 2:2.

5. Soz. 1.18.1–4. On holy men versus philosophers, cf. Rufinus *HM* 28; Palladius *HL* 38.11; Epiphan. *Pan.* 66.11; Cassian *Coll.* 15.3, 5.21.

6. Soc. 1.11. Scholarship has not succeeded in identifying this Paphnutius; cf. Thelamon *PC* 464. Galerius Maximianus, Caesar 293–311, was a vigorous persecutor and uncle of the equally notable persecutor Maximinus Daia (Caesar 305–313), of whom Eusebius mentions that he mutilated Christians and gouged out their eyes (*Church History* 8.14.13). Rufinus may have confused the two names.

7. Rufinus gives the earliest biographical details about Spyridon of Trimithus, but was he at the Council of Nicaea? Cf. E. Honigmann, "La liste originale des Pères de Nicée," *Byzantion* 14 (1939), 59–61. Soc. 1.12; Soz. 1.11.

It was not uncommon for bishops to work at various trades to support themselves (in order to remain independent of the rich and able to admonish them): cf. Epiphan. *Pan.* 70.2.2, 80.4.7–8, 80.5.5–6.4.

On the theme of malefactors and enemies magically or miraculously immobilized in pagan and Christian (especially monastic) literature, cf. A.-J. Festugière, "Lieux communs littéraires et thèmes de folk-lore dans l'hagiographie primitive," *Wiener Studien* 73 (1960), 123–152, esp. 146–148. It is a commonplace that the holy person gives the thief what he came for: cf. Thelamon *PC* 409.

8. On the custom of depositing money in temples, cf. Cicero *Laws* 2.16.41; Xenophon *Anabasis* 5.3.6; Plautus *Bacchides* 306–307. On consulting the dead about missing deposits, cf. Herodotus 5.92; *Apophthegmata Patrum* 7 (*PG* 65.265–266); Augustine *De cura gerenda pro mortuis* 11.13.

9. There were actually only two bishops who were exiled with Arius: Secundus of Ptolemais and Theonas of Marmarica; cf. Philostorgius 1.9; Theodoret 1.7.15. For a list of twenty-two "Arianizing" bishops (at Nicaea?), cf. Philostorgius 1.8ᵃ. The tradition of six bishops who supported Arius is echoed in Theodoret 1.5.5 and 1.7.14. Cf. also Soc. 1.8.31–33; Soz. 1.21.1–5.

10. "ex alia subsistentia vel substantia," translating ἐξ ἑτέρας ὑποστάσεως ἢ οὐσίας. Marius Victorinus seems to have been the first to translate ὑπόστασις as *subsistentia* (hesitantly), Rufinus the first to apply the translation to the Creed of Nicaea. Cf. M. Victorinus *Adversus Arium* 2.4 and 3.4. On the distinction between ὑπόστασις and οὐσία, cf. J. Hammerstaedt, "Hypostasis," *RAC* 16.986–1035; Hanson 181–190. Rufinus in translating Gregory Naz. *Or.* 2.36 had rendered ὑπόστασις as "subsistentia ac persona," so that the reader would not

confuse it with *substantia*; cf. C. Moreschini, "Rufino traduttore di Gregorio Nazianzeno," *AAAd* 31 (1987), 1.236. The earlier Latin translations of the Creed had made heavy weather of this passage; cf. *EOMIA* 1.298–299. Rufinus's solution was generally accepted, and *subsistentia* became part of the technical vocabulary of Latin theology. See also note 42. His version of the Creed is, mysteriously, almost the same as that known as the "Interpretatio Caeciliani" (*EOMIA* 1.106 and 108), which according to Schwartz (1.204–206) was produced later.

For the original text of the Creed of Nicaea, cf. *DEC* 1.5.

11. For the original Canons of Nicaea, cf. *DEC* 1.6–16. For commentary, see Hefele-Leclercq 1.503–620. For the various Latin versions, cf. *EOMIA* 1.112–143 and 178–243. For commentary on these versions, see Hefele-Leclercq 1.1139–1176; Schwartz 4.159–275.

Rufinus's version is independent of the earlier one to which the Canons of Sardica became attached. It abridges and occasionally glosses the original, and the numeration is slightly different. It does not include the final Canon 20 of the original (against kneeling for prayer on Sundays and during Eastertide). Pope Innocent (402–417) had it excerpted, together with the Creed, under the title *Abbreviatio*, and in that form it often appears in the early Latin canonical collections. Cf. F. Maassen, *Geschichte der Quellen und der Literatur des canonischen Rechts* (Gratz, 1870), 33–34; Hefele-Leclercq 1.1163–1165; Schwartz 4.205, 4.218.

12. "Et ut apud Alexandriam vel in urbe Roma vetusta consuetudo servetur, quia vel ille Aegypti vel hic suburbicariarum ecclesiarum sollicitudinem gerat."

This corresponds to the first part of the original Canon 6, which runs: Τὰ ἀρχαῖα ἔθη κρατείτω τὰ ἐν Ἀιγύπτῳ καὶ Λιβύῃ καὶ Πενταπόλει, ὥστε τὸν Ἀλεξανδρείας ἐπίσκοπον πάντων ἔχειν τὴν ἐξουσίαν, ἐπειδὴ καὶ τῷ ἐν τῇ Ῥώμῃ ἐπισκόπῳ τὸ τοιοῦτον σύνηθές ἐστιν. Ὁμοίως δὲ καὶ κατὰ τὴν Ἀντιόχειαν καὶ ἐν ταῖς ἄλλαις ἐπαρχίαις τὰ πρεσβεῖα σώζεσθαι ταῖς ἐκκλησίαις. ["The ancient customs of Egypt, Libya, and Pentapolis shall be maintained, according to which the bishop of Alexandria has authority over all these places, since a similar custom exists with reference to the bishop of Rome. Similarly in Antioch and the other provinces the prerogatives of the churches are to be preserved" (*DEC* translation)].

Schwartz (4.205) attributes the "suburbicarian gloss" to Rufinus himself; J. Gaudemet thinks it precedes him; cf. *L'église dans l'empire romain* (Paris, 1958), 445. The gloss is based on the words "Egypt, Libya, and Pentapolis" in the original canon, which make it clear that the (civil) diocese of Egypt is being referred to, not just the province. Now a diocese was normally governed by a "vicar," but the diocese of Italy was divided into the two regions of *Italia annonaria* to the north, under the *vicarius Italiae*, and the *suburbicariae regiones* of the center and south, which were under the *vicarius urbis*. In a sense, then, the southern half of Italy could be seen as equivalently a diocese, as being under its own vicar, and Rome was located within it (although it was governed by the *praefectus urbis*). Cf. Hefele-Leclercq 1.1182–1202, esp. 1.1197–1198.

Since the original canon grounds itself upon the practice of the church of Rome in acknowledging the authority of the bishop of Alexandria over an entire (civil) diocese, Rufinus in his gloss defines more precisely which "diocese" the bishop of Rome governs, sharply reducing thereby the extent of papal authority set out in the earlier Latin version of this canon: "Ecclesia Romana semper habuit primatus, teneat autem et Aegyptus ut episcopus Alexandriae omnium habeat potestatem, quoniam et Romano episcopo haec est consuetudo" (*EOMIA* 1.121). Schwartz (4.205) thinks that Rufinus is deliberately confining papal authority to the region of Italy south of his own homeland, perhaps in reply to the anti-Origenist pressure he had felt from that quarter.

13. "Paulianists" are followers of Paul of Samosata, the third-century bishop of Antioch deposed for denying Christ's divinity. Rufinus associates with him Photinus, bishop of Sirmium (ca. 344–351), who was accused of holding similar views.

14. Helena (ca. 249–329) visited Syria and Palestine toward the end of her life in order to see the holy places. The only useful account of this visit is Eusebius *VC* 3.42–43 (no mention of the cross). Cf. R. Klein, "Helena," *RAC* 14 (1988) 355–375, esp. 367–369.

Cyril of Jerusalem, in his letter of 351 to the emperor Constantius, speaks in part 3 of the Savior's cross having been found in Jerusalem in Constantine's time, the divine grace having granted the discovery of the holy places to him who sought them rightly; he does not mention Helena. Cf. J. Rupp, *Cyrilli Opera* (Munich, 1860) 2.434–436.

The tradition of Helena finding the cross is first found in Ambrose *De obitu Theodosii* 45–47 (composed in 395). Rufinus is the first to tell the story about the sick woman; in Ambrose's account it is the inscription on the true cross which allows Helena to identify it. Both agree that Helena made gifts for her son from the nails; in Ambrose they are a bridle and a diadem. Soc. 1.17; Soz. 2.1; Theodoret 1.18.

15. "Constantinus pietate fretus Sarmatas, Gothos aliasque barbaras nationes . . . in solo proprio armis edomuit." Cf. Orosius 7.28.29, where the emperor defeats the Goths "in ipso barbarici soli sinu, hoc est in Sarmatarum regione" after closing the pagan temples. The Goths were beaten in 332 and the Sarmatians in 334.

16. Cf. [Athan.] *Life of Antony* 81.

17. The ascription to Athanasius of the Greek *Life of Antony* is doubtful; cf. Barnes 240. The modern edition is by G. J. M. Bartelink, *Vie d'Antoine. Athanase* (Paris, 1994). It was very soon translated into Latin twice: one version was by Evagrius of Antioch ca. 370 (printed in *PG* 26.837–978); the other translation, an anonymous one, was perhaps done earlier. The modern edition is again that of Bartelink, *Vita di Antonio* (Milan, 1974). Cf. A. di Berardino, *Patrology* (Westminster, MD, 1991), 4.206–207.

18. On the mission of Thomas to Parthia: Eusebius *Church History* 3.1.1. On India and Thomas: *Acts of Thomas* 1; Chromatius of Aquileia *Sermo* 26.4. On India and Bartholomew: Eusebius *Church History* 5.10.3; Jerome *De viris illustribus* 36.

To understand Rufinus's geographical description, it is helpful to remember that Africa and the subcontinent of India were commonly thought to be connected by a land bridge. "India" could not only have its modern meaning but refer as well to the interior regions of Africa in and beyond Ethiopia and to the coastal area of Himyar (Yemen). Cf. A. Dihle, "Umstrittene Daten" *Untersuchungen zum Auftreten der Griechen am Roten Meer* (*Wissenschaftliche Abhandlungen der Arbeitsgemeinschaft für Forschung des Landes Nordrhein-Westfalen* 32 [1965]), 36–64. On the confusion between India and Ethiopia: *Expositio totius mundi et gentium* 35; Cosmas Indicopleustes 2.48. Rufinus seems to have invented the terms *India citerior* and *India ulterior* (translated here as "Hither India" and "Further India"): Dihle, "Umstrittene Daten," 41. The custom of dividing India already existed, however; *Expositio* 16 and 17 speaks of *India maior* and *India minor*. By *India citerior*, Rufinus seems to mean the Red Sea coastal area, while *India ulterior* refers to Aksum: Dihle, "Umstrittene Daten," 44.

On the adventurer Metrodorus, see Ammianus Marcellinus 25.4.23; Cedrenus 295AB.

Cf. Soc. 1.19; Soz. 2.24; Theodoret 1.23; Philostorgius 2.6.

19. Rufinus does not name the port where Meropius's ship had put in for provisions (Dihle, "Umstrittene Daten," 46, conjectures Adulis), but he evidently thinks of it as somewhere still in "Further India," since he is telling of how that land came to be evangelized. The evidence suggests that the kingdom referred to is Aksum (in modern-day Ethiopia): cf. ibid., 49; Klein, 239–240.

On trade between Rome and Aksum, cf. Eusebius *VC* 4.7.1 (Indian and Ethiopian envoys bearing gifts for Constantine); *C. Th.* 12.12.2 (dated 356); A. Dihle, "Die entdeckungsgeschichtlichen Voraussetzungen des Indienhandels der römischen Kaiserzeit," *ANRW* 2.9.2 (1978), 546–580.

The anti-Roman practice described by Rufinus is otherwise unheard-of, and the attack on the ship seems an act of piracy rather than policy: Thelamon *PC* 66. Jerome mentions the dangers of Red Sea voyages in *Ep.* 125.3.

20. "nuper sacerdotium susceperat." The chronology does not square with that suggested by Constantius's letter to the rulers of Aksum (Athan. *Apologia ad Constantium* 31), which does indeed say that Athanasius ordained Frumentius bishop of their realm but implies that this took place recently: they are to send Frumentius to be examined by George of Alexandria to make sure his teaching is orthodox before he has a chance to corrupt the Christians in their country. Athanasius, it says, is after all a convicted criminal. Now Athanasius became bishop in 328, but the letter is from the year 356. Thelamon therefore conjectures that Rufinus has deliberately falsified the chronology in order to make it appear that the mission to Aksum took place in Constantine's time rather than Constantius's, Constantine being one of the great heroes of his history, while his son was a deluded persecutor (Thelamon *PC* 62). Klein 240 thinks that the chronology can still be squared if "susceperat" is understood as Athanasius's resumption of episcopal office after one of his exiles—that is, in 338 or 346. But that is stretching things a bit.

21. Rufinus's is the earliest extant account of the conversion of the *Hiberi* or Georgians. Thelamon has conjectured that behind the story of the *captiva* who introduced Christianity to their land there lies a typical Georgian narrative of the foundation of a cult or shrine. Such accounts often feature a woman called a *kadag* who is a possessed intermediary between the divine and human realms and who is often referred to as "captive" or "seized." Certain elements in Rufinus's story, such as the taking of sick children around to the neighbors, the strict separation of the sexes (the king evangelizes the men and the queen the women), the distinction between the exterior and interior architecture of the church, and the mysterious hanging column, have a peculiarly Georgian ring. But we cannot say how Christianity was really introduced to that country, since however it happened, the story came to be told in the usual Georgian fashion, in which the new cult was authenticated by the miraculous activities of the shaman. Rufinus took and retailed the account at face value, although its setting within Constantine's reign may be his own contribution. Cf. Thelamon *PC* 93–119; Soc. 1.20; Soz. 2.7; Theodoret 1.24.

On Georgia and the history of its Christianization, cf. O. Lordkipanidse and H. Brakmann, "Iberia II (Georgien)," *RAC* 17 (1995), 12–106, esp. 34–35 and 40–57. There is some evidence of Christian burial sites in Georgia from the second and third centuries, but there is no agreement about when during the next century the monarchy became Christian; some would hold for 325–

330, although ca. 337 or 355–356 seems more likely. It was the fourth century that offered conditions favorable to this conversion. The forty-year truce between Rome and Persia concluded in 299 put Armenia and Georgia within the Roman sphere of influence and provided that the Georgian kings should receive their tokens of rule from the Romans. The religious influence of the Sassanids thereby ended in Georgia. Sapor II (309–379) strove from 339 on to regain the lost territory, while Constantius for his part worked to keep the Iberian king Meribanes III loyal (Ammianus Marcellinus 21.6.8). Jovian's treaty with the Persians did not include the renunciation of power over Georgia. But in 369 Sapor drove out the Iberian king Sauromaces II, who returned the following year escorted by a Roman army. Thereafter, however, Georgia, like Armenia, became divided gradually into Roman and Persian spheres of influence.

There has been little critical discussion of Thelamon's theory of the origin of Rufinus's account, perhaps because there seems no way of proving or disproving it; there is no other independent source against which to check Rufinus. Lordkipanidse simply says that there is no reason why he should not be taken at face value, once it is noted that he has probably followed his usual inclination to shift edifying material from Constantius's reign to that of his father's (Lordkipanidse and H. Brakman, "Iberia II (Georgien)," 51). Later Georgian tradition gives names to the chief characters in the story; the captive woman becomes the famous Nino, whose adventures are woven from missionary fable and genuine history, while the king is called Mirian, usually identified with the Meribanes who reigned during Constantius's time (Ammianus Marcellinus 21.6.8). His conversion fostered the growth of the central royal government, which confiscated the pagan temple properties and gave them to the nobles and the church; the ancient Georgian sources give evidence of how actively the monarchy and the nobility propagated Christianity and of the resistance they encountered from the mountain folk and those among the ruling class who opposed the strengthening of the central government. The conversion of the royal house was not in any case the same as the Christianization of Georgia as a whole, nor is there any reason to suppose that only one individual was responsible for it. There is good evidence of other missionary work being done there during the fourth century in the regions near Colchis and Armenia.

22. The *comes domesticorum* commanded the court garrison; the *dux limitis* was in charge of troops in frontier districts.

On Bacurius, cf. Ammianus Marcellinus 31.12.16; Zosimus 4.57.3 and 4.58; Soc. 1.20.20; Libanius Ep. 1043–1044, 1060; *PLRE* 1.144; D. Hoffmann, "Wadomar, Bacurius, und Hariulf," *Museum Helveticum* 35 (1978), 307–318. Libanius, in his letters, seems to consider him a fellow pagan.

23. On Constantia, cf. Hanson 28; Stein-Palanque 1.108; *PLRE* 1.221. She and her niece Constantina were sometimes confused (e.g., Philostorgius 1.9).

Constantine invited Arius to court in a letter of November 27, 327 (Opitz *Urk.* 29). Arius's creed is Opitz *Urk.* 30 (translated in R. Williams, *Arius* 255–256). He was restored to communion by a Council of Nicomedia in 327 or 328, but neither Alexander nor later Athanasius would take him back. Constantine called Arius to court a second time in 333. It is not known where he was or what he did in the interval, but he may have spent some time in Libya (ibid., 75–77). The creed referred to earlier was probably presented at his first interview. The reason for the second was that Arius had written to Constantine complaining about not being received back into his home church, and the emperor thought he was threatening schism (Opitz *Urk.* 34.5).

However he did it, Arius cleared himself well enough to persuade Constantine to put his rehabilitation on the agenda of the Council of Jerusalem, which met in 335 to celebrate the Dedication of the Church of the Holy Sepulchre. On this large and lavishly conducted council, cf. Eusebius *VC* 4.43–48. The emperor's letter to it which Rufinus mentions has not survived but is referred to in the council's own letter, reproduced in Athan. *De synodis* 21.

The impression Rufinus gives of the freedom Constantine granted the council to judge Arius ("si expositionem fidei eius probarent") is not to be trusted. The council's letter makes it clear that the emperor had vouched for Arius's orthodoxy in his own letter to it (Athan. *De synodis* 21.4) and urged his readmission to communion; it also says furthermore that it is appending a copy of the emperor's letter, which makes it likely that its summary of that letter is accurate. Cf. Soz. 2.27.

24. On Constantine's final days, cf. G. Fowden, "The Last Days of Constantine: Oppositional Versions and Their Influence," *JRS* 84 (1994), 146–170.

Constantine died on May 22, 337, having in 335 appointed his three surviving sons—Constantine, Constantius, and Constans—and his nephew Dalmatius "Caesars" over the four parts of the empire. His body was conveyed to Constantinople, and in due course Constantius arrived from Antioch. The course of events immediately following is not altogether clear, but Dalmatius and all other possible rivals for power were killed, probably by soldiers determined to maintain the dynasty. On September 9, 337, the three brothers were proclaimed Augusti in Pannonia and reallocated the empire among themselves. On the sources, cf. Paschoud 1.246–247; Stein-Palanque 1.131–132; Klein 200.

The story about the presbyter and the will appears first in Rufinus, but it probably precedes him; cf. Klein 2. In Philostorgius 2.16, the will is entrusted to Eusebius of Nicomedia.

25. Rufinus's chronology is badly and perhaps deliberately muddled. Alexander of Alexandria had died and been succeeded by Athanasius in 328. Athanasius was condemned by the Council of Tyre in 335 and banished by Constantine to Gaul. Despite the urging of the Council of Jerusalem, which was in effect a continuation of that of Tyre, the Alexandrian church did not welcome Arius upon his return, riots broke out, and Constantine called him back to Constantinople (Soc. 1.37.1–2), where the council to which Rufinus refers met in 336. Constantine, despite what Rufinus says, was very much alive during the whole episode, but Rufinus may well have falsified the chronology in order to spare him the shame of having exiled Athanasius and brought Arius back (cf. Thelamon *PC* 35).

The story of Arius's death was repeated endlessly, beginning with Athan. *De morte Arii* 2–4 and *Ad episcopos Aegypti* 19. This sort of death was regarded as a special sign of divine wrath; cf., for example, 2 Macc. 9:5–28; Acts 12:23; Josephus *Antiquities* 17.168–70; Lactantius *De mortibus* 33; Eusebius *Church History* 2.10.7; Ammianus Marcellinus 14.11.24–25.

It has sometimes been doubted that Alexander of Byzantium/Constantinople was still alive at the time, but Barnes 213 has shown that he was.

26. Alexander died on April 17, 328, and Athanasius succeeded him on June 8. Stories of heroes acting out their future roles while children are common enough; for example, see Herodotus 1.114–115; *Historia Augusta* Severus 1.4 and Albinus 5.2; Photius *Bibl.* cod. 258; Thelamon *PC* 337. Cf. Soc. 1.15; Soz. 2.17.6–10.

27. Acts 9:16.

28. Ps. 2:1–2.

29. Ps. 27:3.

30. Constantine the Younger and Constans had quarreled, perhaps about the supervision which the older brother was trying to exercise over the younger, and in 340 Constantine invaded the other's territory. Constans from Naissus sent troops to ambush him, and he was killed. For the sources cf. Paschoud 1.248.

The words "Constantius orientis regnum solus obtinuit Constantino fratre . . . interfecto" suggest that Constantius was somehow subject to his older brother, and they seem related to Themistius's claim that he received an unfair share of his father's empire (*Or.* 2.38c). Klein 76 and 201 says that Constans got Thrace (including Constantinople) in the initial allotment among the three brothers but ceded it to Constantius in 339 in return for support against Constantine. Constantine's guardianship over Constans is discussed by J. R. Palanque, "Collégialité et partage dans l'empire romain aux IV$^e$ et V$^e$ siècle,"

*Révue des études anciennes* 46 (1944), 54–56. Schwartz, 3.268–269, on the other hand, believes that Thrace belonged to Constantius from the outset.

31. Cf. note 25; despite what Rufinus says, the Council of Tyre was held in 335 during Constantine's reign, and it was Constantine who banished him at the end of it. Rufinus may simply be trying to shift the responsibility for this act onto his son.

The count mentioned is Flavius Dionysius, former governor of Syria. Archelaus was count of Oriens (?) in 340 and governor of Phoenicia in 335; cf. *PLRE* 1.100. On the council, cf. Eusebius *VC* 4.41–42; Athan. *Apol. contra Arianos* 71–86; *P. Lond.* 1914, in H. I. Bell, *Jews and Christians in Egypt* (London, 1924), 53–71; Epiphan. *Pan.* 68.8–9; Ammianus Marcellinus 15.7.7–8; Soc. 1.28–32; Soz. 2.25; Theodoret 1.29–31; Philostorgius 2.11; Hanson, 246–262; Barnes, 22–24.

As Rufinus indicates, the charges against Athanasius were disciplinary, not doctrinal, whatever the ulterior motives of his opponents may have been. But Rufinus passes over in silence the main accusation that he had used violence against clergy who had refused to accept his authority because they considered his ordination invalid.

Athanasius had previously been charged with the murder of Arsenius and had cleared himself with Constantine in 334 by producing his alleged victim alive and having his identity confirmed by the bishop of Tyre (Athan. *Apol. contra Arianos* 63.4–70). The story is the sort that easily gets repeated out of context (as in fact happens in Epiphan. *Pan.* 68.10.1–2), so when it shows up again at the Council of Tyre, one's first inclination is to discount it as an errant tale. But Sozomen also relates it, along with the story about the woman, in his account of the council, and he goes on to remark that the latter story is not included in the acts (2.25.11). That implies that the story about Arsenius was, and this squares with what Athanasius himself says about Arsenius being present at the council in refutation of the murder charge (*Apol. contra Arianos* 72.2). Evidently then the old murder charge was raked up again (as Sozomen in fact plainly says in 2.25.7). Small wonder that Constantine was persuaded of the council's unfairness when he heard of it (Athan. *Apol. contra Arianos* 9.5). It strengthens the general impression that the Council of Tyre was procedurally untidy, often disorderly, and occasionally chaotic. The unruliness of Athanasius's suffragans made matters worse; the behavior of Paphnutius toward Maximus of Jerusalem is quite in line with what we read elsewhere (Epiphan. *Pan.* 68.8.2–5). Despite what Rufinus says, Maximus voted to depose Athanasius (Soc. 2.24.3).

10.16: "magicae artis gratia": "for magical purposes" (*not* "by magical means"). The magical use of the bodily parts of persons put to death was well enough known (cf. *RE* 14.332–333), and the charge of magic against Athanasius was long remembered (Ammianus Marcellinus 15.7.8).

Despite what Rufinus says, Athanasius did not choose voluntary exile but escaped from Tyre secretly by night and sailed to Constantinople, where he accosted the emperor and persuaded him to summon his opponents to court and let him meet them there. Six of the leading bishops arrived shortly and brought a new charge against Athanasius: that he had threatened to interrupt the grain shipments from Egypt to the capital. The hearing turned stormy, and in the end Athanasius lost both his temper and his case; Constantine banished him to Trier on November 7, 335.

32. The chronology here is sheer fantasy. Athanasius returned from exile to Alexandria on November 23, 337, after Constantine's death and upon the initiative of his oldest son, who restored all banished bishops to their cities. His life was never in any danger. He was deposed again, however, by the Council of Antioch of 338/9 (on charges of violence and improper resumption of his see). The council appointed Gregory the Cappadocian to replace him, an attempt was made to arrest him, and he escaped and sailed to Italy on April 16, 339.

The emperor Constans was persuaded to take up the cause of Athanasius and other exiled Eastern bishops. The Council of Sardica of 343, which he summoned to review their cases, cleared the exiles and ordered their return, but Athanasius did not enter Alexandria again until October of 346, after Constans had written to his brother threatening to invade his realm, if necessary, to restore him. There are different versions of his letter in Soc. 2.22.5, Theodoret 2.8.55–56, and Philostorgius 3.12.

Rufinus's description of Athanasius's concealment corresponds rather to the period of 356 to 362, when Athanasius was being hunted by Constantius and remained in hiding in his city or nearby until the emperor's death. For a different version of how he remained hidden, cf. Palladius *HL* 63 (cf. Athan. *Festal Index* 32).

33. Widespread dissatisfaction with Constans's rule led to the usurpation of Magnentius, one of his generals, in January of 350. Constans was killed and Magnentius began sounding out possible dissidents in the other half of the empire, among them Athanasius (Athan. *Apol. ad Const.* 6–10). Nothing came of it but the civil war in which Magnentius was finally defeated, after heavy losses on both sides, and died in 353.

When Constantius arrived in Sirmium in 351 to prosecute the war, its bishop, Photinus, had long been notorious for his denial of the preexistence of Christ, a doctrine commonly thought to have been derived from Marcellus of Ancyra. A council met in Sirmium that year and condemned Photinus,

Marcellus, and Athanasius. Its synodical letter has not survived, so we cannot tell directly how the council associated the three, but Sulpicius Severus suggests that the condemnation of Marcellus (as Photinus's master) was seen by many as effectively annulling the Council of Sardica, which had cleared him. If so, then Athanasius's absolution by the same council was void, and his deposition by the Council of Antioch remained valid, particularly if, as was rumored, he had himself suspended Marcellus from communion (*Chron.* 2.37.1–5).

Liberius of Rome in 352 or 353 convoked an Italian synod to consider a reply to the Council of Sirmium based on the opposing dossiers in the case; it cleared Athanasius but requested a larger council to meet in Aquileia to review the issue. Athanasius himself sent a delegation to Constantius; it was unsuccessful. The council requested for Aquileia met instead in Arles, where the court was, in 353. The letter of the Council of Sirmium was presented to it, and those present were told to subscribe it under threat of exile. Paulinus of Trier asked that doctrine be first discussed in order to make sure that all those present were fit to be judges, but his request was refused and he was banished. Constantius was then asked by Liberius to call another council (Hilary *Frag.* A VII 6); it met in Milan in 355, with the same subscription being demanded of those present.

Eusebius of Vercelli tried again to put doctrine on the agenda by declaring himself ready to subscribe what was demanded if everyone would first subscribe the Creed of Nicaea. Dionysius of Milan was just about to do so when Valens of Mursa, one of Athanasius's enemies, snatched pen and paper away, shouting that he was out of order (Hilary *Ad Const. August.* 3(8).1). The story was widely circulated, and from then on the success of Athanasius's attempt to identify his cause with that of Nicene orthodoxy was assured.

Eusebius, Dionysius, and Lucifer of Cagliari, who refused to subscribe, were exiled; Eusebius went to Scythopolis in Palestine and Lucifer to Germanicia in Syria, but both seemed to move around a good deal in the East during their time there. Constantius's officials carried the synodical of the Council of Sirmium around to the bishops who had not attended the aforementioned councils and demanded their subscription (cf. Barnes 115–116). Hilary of Poitiers was banished to Phrygia after the Council of Béziers in 356. We do not know why or when Rhodanius of Toulouse was exiled.

Gregory had died in 345 before Athanasius returned to Alexandria; George the Cappadocian was appointed by the Council of Antioch of 349 to replace Athanasius but could not enter his city until a year after Athanasius had left it in February of 356 to escape arrest. Constantius's letter to the Alexandrians leaves no doubt that he considered Athanasius worthy of death for his crimes

(Athan. *Apol. ad Const.* 30). On measures taken against those loyal to Athanasius, cf. Athan. *Festal Index* 29–32.

34. Constantius became convinced that the rifts in the church, including those caused by the new "anomoean" doctrine (of the dissimilarity of God the Father and the Son), could only be repaired by a general council, and he called one to meet in Nicomedia in 358. But the city was destroyed by earthquake that summer, and by the following summer it had been decided to hold separate councils in Ariminum and Seleucia (in Isauria). The court had decided to press the bishops to accept a new creed which would outlaw the use of the controversial word *ousia* in statements of faith, thus rescinding the Creed of Nicaea (see J. N. D. Kelly, *Early Christian Creeds* [London, 1972³], 289–291).

The Council of Ariminum met in July with over four hundred attending. Due largely perhaps to Hilary of Poitier's correspondence from exile, the Westerners now appreciated the importance of the Creed of Nicaea, and most of them refused to subscribe to the new one. A minority of about eighty seceded, each side sending a delegation to court, as the councils had been instructed. Constantius refused to receive the majority delegates and wore them down through tedium and fear until they gave in and signed his creed on October 10. When they returned to Ariminum the majority refused them communion, but the praetorian prefect Flavius Taurus told the bishops they could not go home until they signed. The opposition gradually dwindled to twenty, who finally gave in when told they might formulate their subscriptions as they liked. The signature was not then, as now, a bare name, but a complete sentence or sentences resuming the body of the agreement to which it was attached. It was regarded as an authentic interpretation of it, as Valens of Mursa, one of the Arian leaders there, had been sharply reminded by the emperor himself when he had tried to omit a key phrase in his own subscription of the new creed the previous May (Epiphan. *Pan.* 73.22.6). Thus the council fathers were told they might include in their subscriptions whatever they felt was lacking in the main body of the new creed. Valens himself wrote in his that the Son of God was not a creature like other creatures, the ambiguity of which was evidently not noticed by the others until later, when the rumor began spreading that they had signed an Arian creed. After they had authorized a new delegation to court, they were allowed to break up. Rufinus's story of how the majority was tricked is thus quite wide of the mark.

The Council of Seleucia got under way late in September with 160 in attendance, and as in Ariminum, the majority refused to accept the new creed, taking its stand instead on the Creed of the Dedication Council of Antioch of 341 (on this creed, see Kelly, *Early Christian Creeds*, 268–271); the minority in favor of the new creed seceded, and both sides sent a delegation to court. The majority delegates were as stubborn as their Ariminum counterparts had been, but the court could now represent them as recalcitrants hindering the work of church unity, and on the last day of the year they finally yielded and signed. Cf. Hilary *Frag.* A.V, VI, VIII, IX, B.VIII; Athan. *De synodis* 8–12; Jerome *contra Luciferianos* 18; Augustine *Opus imperfectum contra Iulianum* 1.75; Sulpicius Severus *Chron.* 2.41.1–2.45.4; Soc. 2.37; Soz. 4.16–19, 4.22–23; Theodoret 2.18–21; 2.26.4–11; Philostorgius 4.10–11; *EOMIA* 1.541; Hefele-Leclercq 1.929–955; Barnes 144–148.

35. Liberius succeeded Julius in 352. He refused to condemn Athanasius and was banished to Beroea in Thrace. There he eventually yielded and signed the condemnation together with some creed (which? cf. Hanson 358–362, and H. C. Brennecke, *Hilarius von Poitiers und die Bischofsopposition gegen Konstantius II* [Berlin, 1984], 273–297), and was allowed to return to Rome in 357. See also 10.28. His archdeacon Felix was consecrated to replace him by three bishops at court, including the powerful Acacius of Caesarea (Jerome *De viris illustribus* 98). The "connivance" Rufinus mentions refers to the oath which had been taken by the Roman clergy not to accept another bishop while Liberius lived and which most of them broke (Jerome *Chron.* 349; *Collectio Avellana* 1.2). His judgment about Felix still stands in sharp contrast to that of Athanasius, who tarred him with the Arian brush (*Hist. Arian.* 75.3), but it is supported by Theodoret 2.17.3.

36. Maximus of Jerusalem had offended Acacius by receiving Athanasius after condemning him at the Council of Tyre, but he may have died before he could be deposed; it was reported, however, that Acacius had driven him from Jerusalem and ordained Cyril in his place (Soc. 2.38.2). The report in Jerome *Chron.* 348 is probably false; cf. G. Bardy, "Cyrille de Jérusalem," *DHGE* 13.1181–1186.

Rufinus's characterization of George is quite accurate; his greed knew no bounds (cf. Ammianus Marcellinus 22.11.3–10; Epiphan. *Pan.* 76.1).

37. Eudoxius got himself elected irregularly to succeed Leontius of Antioch in 357, but the following year he had to withdraw from the city when Constantius made it clear he did not support him. He was transferred to Constantinople by the council meeting there in 360, and Meletius, from Sebaste in Armenia or Beroea in Syria, was chosen by popular acclaim bishop of Antioch. His preaching so offended the Homoeans, though, that he was promptly banished to Armenia and replaced by Arius's old associate Euzoius. The offending homily is in Epiphan. *Pan.* 73.29–33. On the divisions in Antioch, cf. K. M. Spoerl, "The Schism at Antioch since Cavallera," in *Arianism after Arius*, ed. M. R. Barnes and D. H. Williams (Edinburgh, 1993), 101–126.

38. Ps. 34:15. On the three groups in question, cf. Hanson 557–636, 760–772. On Aetius, cf. T. A. Kopecek, *A History of Neo-Arianism* (Cambridge,

MA, 1979), 61–132. On Eunomius, cf. Kopecek, *A History of Neo-Arianism*, 145–176, 299–543; R. P. Vaggione, *Eunomius: The Extant Works* (Oxford, 1987). On Eunomius's leprosy, cf. Philostorgius 10.6. On heresy as leprosy, cf. Quodvultdeus *Liber promissionum* 2.6.10–11 (*CCL* 60).

On the tangled history of Paul of Constantinople and Macedonius, cf. Barnes 212–217. When Alexander of Constantinople died in 337, Paul was consecrated irregularly but expelled by Constantius and replaced by Eusebius of Nicomedia. Eusebius died in 341. Paul's supporters tried to restore him, but the Arians installed Macedonius, who battled with Paul's supporters throughout his tenure. That came to an end when he was deposed by the Council of Constantinople of 360 and replaced by Eudoxius, although the official grounds of dismissal were disciplinary, not doctrinal (Soc. 2.42.3).

39. Constantius, who was without a male heir, proclaimed his cousin Julian Caesar on November 6, 355, and sent him to Gaul under careful supervision. Julian turned out to be an excellent and popular administrator and general, to the alarm of Constantius, who ordered him to send units to the East for the Persian war in the winter of 359/60. The units rebelled and declared Julian Augustus in February of 360. Constantius was on the march to engage him in battle when he died at Mopsucrenae on November 3, 361. Cf. Jones 1.117, 1.120; Paschoud 2.83–88.

40. On Julian's edict allowing the bishops to return (issued in 360 before Constantius's death?), cf. Barnes 154.

Lucifer was represented at the Council of Alexandria by two deacons, not one; cf. *Tomus ad Antiochenos* 9.

The factions in Antioch were: those loyal to Bishop Eustathius, deposed in 327, who were led by Paulinus; those loyal to Meletius; the Arians under Euzoius. There was also a group led by the presbyter Vitalis, who represented Apollinarian views, but they may not have worshiped separately. Cf. Epiphan. *Pan.* 77.20.3–24.2; R. Devreesse, *Le patriarcat d'Antioche* (Paris, 1945), 20–21. When Rufinus refers to the parties at variance, he means the first two.

Lucifer and Eusebius had not been exiled to Egypt but, rather, during their exile had been able to move around in the East (cf. note 33); Eusebius by this time had already visited Antioch (10.31).

41. When news of Constantius's death reached Alexandria, George was put into prison, from which he was later dragged by a mob and lynched (on December 24, 361). Athanasius returned to his city on February 21, 362, and lost little time in summoning a council which, despite its size (twenty-one attended), proved to be a turning point in the history of the doctrinal alliances of the fourth century. Until recently the *Tomus ad Antiochenos*

(*PG* 26.795–810) was the only primary document of the council thought to have survived (it is a letter composed after the council by a special commission to the church leaders in Antioch concerning the reunification of the parties there). But now the so-called *Epistula Catholica*, traditionally relegated to the spurious Athanasian literature, has been shown to be the first part of its general letter (M. Tetz, "Ein enzyklisches Schreiben der Synode von Alexandrien (362)," *ZNW* 79 (1988), 262–281; the text is edited 271–281). A comparison of the beginning of this letter with the beginning of the account in 10.29 shows that Rufinus had read it (or some version of it); both compare the recent upheavals caused by the heretics to storms from which the church must steer to the desired calm (cf. "quo pacto post haereticorum procellas et perfidiae turbines tranquillitas revocaretur ecclesiae . . . discutiunt" with *Epistula Catholica* (1): ὑπεξελθεῖν καθάπερ ἀπὸ κλύδωνός τινος εἰς λιμένα καὶ σώζειν ἑαυτοὺς ὀφείλετε).

The robe given to the Prodigal Son (Luke 15:22) attracted a rich exegetical tradition, well reviewed by A. M. Piredda, "La veste del figliol prodigo nella tradizione patristica," *Sandalion* 8–9 (1985–1986), 203–242. It was the "first robe," the robe of holiness given to Adam before he sinned and restored to redeemed humanity in Christ. In the Jewish tradition this robe of Adam's is a high-priestly vestment handed down through a succession of eldest sons; according to J. D. M. Derrett, this interpretation reappears in Christian literature with Ambrose ("The Parable of the Prodigal Son: Patristic Allegories and Jewish Midrashim," *Studia Patristica* 10.1 [Berlin, 1970], 219–224). In Ambrose's exposition of the parable, the son is given the robe of wisdom, the priestly garb Rebekah puts on her younger son (*Expos. Luc.* 7.231; *Expos. Ps. CXVIII* 13.15; *De Iac.* 2.2.9). If Rufinus, however, is here summarizing the synodical letter rather than glossing it, then the exposition of the Prodigal Son's robe as a priestly garment antedates Ambrose.

42. Asterius was bishop of Petra; Eusebius, of Vercelli. Sabellius was a third-century heretic whose name had acquired an anti-Trinitarian association. On the translation of οὐσία and ὑπόστασις, see note 10.

"quod quasi tres subsistentes personas significare videretur," translated as "since that would make it clear that three subsistent persons were meant": *quasi* indicates motive or reason here, not comparison; cf. 10.31, where Meletius is said to have retained the loyalty of his followers "quasi pro fide recta."

43. "propriam synodum cum ceteris orientalibus episcopis habuit": for σύνοδος in the sense of an alliance or group of bishops in communion with one another (not noticed in Lampe's *Patristic Greek Lexicon*), cf. Basil *Ep.* 89.1; Epiphan. *Pan.* 71.1.8; 73.34.5.

44. On Lucifer and the schism named after him, cf. Sulpicius Severus *Chron.* 2.45.8; G. F. Diercks, *Luciferi Calaritani Opera Quae Supersunt, CCL* 8 (1978), vii–xxxvii. Jerome says he died during Valentinian's reign (364–375; *De viris illustribus* 95).

On Hilary, cf. J. Doignon, "Hilarius von Poitiers," *RAC* 15 (1991), 139–167. During his exile he remained in touch with the bishops in Gaul and collected the records of the post-Nicene Eastern councils. He was taken to the Council of Seleucia of 359, where he presented his creed and accompanied its delegation to Constantinople. There he protested so vigorously against the course of events in the church that in 360 the emperor told him to return to Gaul. He spent some time in Milan trying unsuccessfully to bring down its Homoean bishop Auxentius, until finally the emperor Valentinian ordered him to leave in 365. He died in 367.

For a bibliography on Hilary, cf. *DHGE* 24 (1993), 459–461. For his works, cf. Doignon, "Hilarius von Poitiers," 141–161. On his activities after returning from exile, Y-.M. Duval, "Vrais et faux problèmes concernant le retour d'exil d'Hilaire de Poitiers et son action en Italie en 360–363," *Athenaeum,* n.s. 48 (1970), 251–275. On his theology, cf. Hanson 471–506. The "books about the faith" which Rufinus mentions may well be the first three books of what is now called his *De Trinitate.*

45. On Julian's concealment of his paganism until he became emperor, cf. Ammianus Marcellinus 21.2.4. He did not forbid Christian youths access to schools, and in fact wanted them to attend so they could learn paganism and be converted to it. But he did rule that teachers had to be pagans; cf. *Ep.* 61; Ammianus 22.10.7 and 25.4.20.

"Militiae cingulum" refers to both the armed and civil services. Julian *Ep.* 83 says that pagans are to be preferred in public office; cf. also Soc. 3.13.1.

Julian's frequent consultation of soothsayers is well attested: cf. Libanius *Or.* 37.5; Ammianus 23.5.10–14; John Chrysostom *De S. Babyla* 77.

Julian's decision to single out Athanasius from among the bishops for exile was crucial, since it lent credence to his long-standing claim that the persecution against him was motivated by the desire to destroy the Christian faith. Cf. Julian *Ep.* 110, 111, 112; Athan. *Historia Acephala* 11; Athan. *Festal Index* 35; Theodoret 3.9; Soz. 4.10.4: Barnes, 158–159.

46. Cf. Ps. 97:7. The facts about the early third-century Antiochene martyr-bishop Babylas are difficult to sort out, but tradition says that he was put to death because he had expelled the emperor Philip from church for murdering a hostage; cf. M. A. Schatkin and P. W. Harkins, *Saint John Chrysostom Apologist* (*The Fathers of the Church* 73 [1985]), 47–70.

Julian's own brother Gallus had been responsible for having Babylas's body moved to the shrine in Daphne in order to convert it to Christian use (Soz. 5.19.12–14). What infuriated Julian was the destruction by fire of the temple of Apollo there shortly after he had reopened the prophetic Castalian spring and had had the martyr's tomb removed. He thought the Christians had done it, and he ordered the main church in Antioch closed; cf. Ammianus Marcellinus 22.12.8–13.3; Julian *Misopogon* 361BC. Cf. John Chrysostom *De S. Babyla* 80–95; Soc. 3.18–19; Soz. 5.19–20; Theodoret 3.10–12; Philostorgius 7.8; *De S. Hieromartyre Babyla* (*PG* 50.532).

Julian appointed Saturninus Secundus Salutius praetorian prefect of Oriens in 361; he accompanied Julian to Antioch in 362. He was a close friend, well educated, and a firm pagan: cf. Paschoud 2.64.

Julian died on June 26, 363. The ancient reports about his death are too numerous to list here, yet even the earliest ones disagreed about whether he had been killed by the enemy or one of his own men, and with what kind of weapon: cf. Paschoud 2.203–205.

47. Dan. 9:24–26; Matt. 24:2; Mark 13:2; Luke 19:44. On Julian's project to rebuild the temple, cf. his *Ep.* 204; Ammianus Marcellinus 23.1.2. The count was Alypius; cf. *PLRE* 1.47; M. Avi-Yonah, *The Jews of Palestine* (Oxford, 1976), 195–196. Jerusalem and its temple had been razed by Titus; Hadrian had later built a temple to Jupiter on the site when he refounded the city as Aelia Capitolina. That temple had been abandoned since Constantine's time. Hadrian's law forbidding the Jews access to Jerusalem had never been totally enforced, but it was repeated by Constantine: cf. Augustine *Sermo* 5.5; Thelamon *PC*, 298–300. On the prophecy about a stone not being left on a stone, cf. Cyril *Catecheses* 15.15. On Jewish women selling their valuables to contribute to the project, cf. Gregory Naz. *Or.* 5.4.

48. The lethal balls of fire are reported by Ammianus Marcellinus 23.1.3. On the whole episode, cf. Gregory Naz. *Or.* 5.3–4; John Chrysostom *Adv. Iudaeos* 5.11, *De S. Babyla* 119; Ambrose *Ep.* 1a(40).12; Soc. 3.20; Soz. 5.22; Theodoret 3.20; Philostorgius 7.9–14; Avi-Yonah, *The Jews of Palestine*, 193–197; S. P. Brock, "Rebuilding of the Temple under Julian: A New Source," *Palestine Exploration Quarterly* (1976), 103–107. The chamber mentioned seems to have been an underground portico built in Herod's time. The fire could have resulted from an explosion of underground gas caused by the earthquake; cf. Thelamon *PC* 306. The cross marked on the spectators' clothing is mentioned in Gregory Naz. *Or.* 5.7

# BOOK II

1. The accession and piety of the sovereign Jovian, and his death.
2. The accession of Valentinian and Valens.
3. The falling asleep of Athanasius and the persecutions of the heretic Lucius.
4. The virtues and miracles of the saints who were in Egypt.
5. The persecution which took place in Edessa.
6. Moses, whom the queen of the Saracens requested as bishop of her people.
7. Didymus, the man of sight in Alexandria.
8. The number of saints among Antony's disciples who even then dwelt in the desert working signs and miracles.
9. The bishops Gregory and Basil of Cappadocia.
10. Bishop Damasus and the intrusion of Ursinus.
11. Bishop Ambrose.
12. The death of Valentinian.
13. The irruption of the Goths through Thrace and the death of the sovereign Valens.
14. The emperor Gratian's appointment of Theodosius to share in his rule, and how after many brave and religious deeds he fell victim to the treachery of the usurper Maximus.

15. The child Valentinian, and how his mother Justina defended the Arian heresy and tried to trouble the churches.

16. The steadfast courage of Benivolus, *magister memoriae.*

17. The triumph of Theodosius over Maximus in avenging Gratian's murder.

18. Theodosius's crime against the Thessalonians and the penance he publicly performed in the presence of the priests.

19. The restitution of the churches which were restored in the East to the Catholics on his account.

20. Apollinaris and his heresy.

21. The succession of bishops in the East.

22. The pagan disorders in Alexandria.

23. The location of the temple of Serapis and its overthrow.

24. The crimes discovered in the pagan temples.

25. Tyrannus, the priest of Saturn and adulterer of almost all of Alexandria.

26. The destruction and origin of Canopus.

27. The churches and martyrs' shrines built on the sites of the idols.

28. The violation of John's tomb and his relics kept in Alexandria.

29. The busts of Serapis scraped off at Alexandria and the sign of Christ put in their place.

30. The bringing to church of the Nile River gauge, the so-called *pêchys.*

31. The death of Valentinian the Younger and accession of Eugenius.

32. The replies of John the monk.

33. The preparations of Theodosius for war against Eugenius, and his victory, the result of prayer rather than power.

34. The death of Theodosius after his victory, and Arcadius and Honorius, his children and heirs to his realm.

**11.1.** After Julian's death a legitimate government was restored to us at last with Jovian; for he appeared at once as emperor, confessor, and averter of the error which had been introduced for evil. For with the army on alert and the barbarian pressing close, our leaders, after discussing the crisis, elected Jovian, who, as he was being seized and taken off to receive the tokens of command, is said to have announced to the army, profaned by Julian's sacrilegious acts, that he could not command them because he was a Christian. They all with one voice are said to have answered, "We are Christians too." Nor would he agree to accept the command before he had heard what they said, according to report. Then God's mercy came to his assistance without delay, and beyond all hope, the enemy having closed them in on all sides with no chance of escape, they suddenly saw envoys approaching from the barbarians who sued for peace, who promised as well to sell food and other provisions to the army, which was prostrate from famine, and who with unbounded kindness corrected the rashness of our people. After he had secured peace for twenty-nine years and returned to Roman soil, and the brighter light which had arisen in the East shone upon our land, he proceeded with all moderation to restore the state after what had seemed great storms, and the care of the churches was not for him a lesser matter. But he did not act heedlessly like Constantius; warned by his predecessor's fall, he summoned Athanasius with a respectful and most dutiful letter. He received from him a creed and a plan for ordering the churches. But an early death ruined these so religious and happy beginnings; eight months after his accession, he died in Cilicia.[1]

**11.2.** Valentinian, whom Julian had expelled from the service because of the faith, succeeded him. But the Lord fulfilled in him what he had promised, restoring to him in the present age even more than a hundredfold; for because he had left the service for the sake of Christ, he received the empire. He took as his partner in government his brother Valens, choosing for himself the West, while he left the East to him. But Valens went off in his fathers' path by supporting the heretics. He sent bishops into exile and while Tatian was governing Alexandria went so far as to hand over presbyters, deacons, and monks to torture and to the flames, and plotted many wicked and cruel deeds against God's church. But all this took place after Athanasius's death, for while he was still alive he was restrained as though by some divine power; he might rage against the others, but against him he dared work no hostile deed.[2]

11.3. During this time, then, in the forty-sixth year of his priesthood, Athanasius, after many struggles and many crowns of suffering, rested in peace. Asked about his successor, he chose Peter to be sharer and partner in his troubles. But Lucius, a bishop of the Arian party, flew at once like a wolf upon the sheep. As for Peter, he immediately boarded a ship and fled to Rome. Lucius, as though the material on which his cruelty could work had been taken from him, became even more savage toward the others and showed himself so bloodthirsty that he did not even try to preserve an appearance of religion. When he first arrived, such enormous and disgraceful deeds were done against the virgins and celibates of the church as are not even recorded in the pagan persecutions. Hence after the banishment and exile of citizens, after the slaughter, torture, and flames with which he brought so many to their death, he turned the weapons of his madness against the monasteries. He laid waste the desert and declared war on the peaceable. He set out likewise to attack the three thousand or more men at the same time who were scattered throughout the whole desert in secret and isolated dwellings, he sent an armed force of cavalry and infantry, he chose tribunes, commanders, and officers as though he were going to do battle against the barbarians. When they arrived, they witnessed a new kind of war: their enemies exposed their necks to the swords and said only, "Friend, for what have you come?"[3]

11.4. At that time those of Antony's disciples living in Egypt and especially in the desert of Nitria who on account of their life and advanced age were considered to be the fathers of the monks were Macarius, Isidore, another Macarius, Heraclides, and Pambo; they were held to be companions in the lives and deeds not of other mortals but of the angels on high. I speak of what I was there to see, and I report the deeds of those whose sufferings I was granted to share. These men led the Lord's army equipped not with mortal weapons but with religious faith, an army which conquered by dying and which, victorious in the shedding of its blood, followed Christ to heaven. While they were in their tents praying and waiting for their killers, a man was brought to them whose limbs, and especially his feet, had long since shriveled up; but when they anointed him with oil in the Lord's name, the soles of his feet were at once made strong. And when they said, "In the name of Jesus Christ, whom Lucius is persecuting, arise, stand on your feet, and return home," he got up at once and, jumping about, blessed God, thus showing that God was really in them.

Now a short time earlier a blind man had asked to be led to Macarius's cell, which was in the desert three days' journey distant. But when his guides had expended much labor in bringing him there, he did not find Macarius at home. Greatly disappointed, he simply could not assuage his unhappiness at lacking the consolation of being healed. But then, plucking up his faith, he said to those who had brought him, "Please take me up to the part of the wall where the elder usually sleeps." When he had been brought there, he put on the palm of his hand a little of the dry mud with which the wall was seen to have been plastered, and asked also that they draw some water from the well from which he usually drank. With the moisture he softened the clod, plastered the mud over his eyes, and washed them with the water that had been drawn, and at once received his sight, so that he was able to return home unassisted. But he did not behave like the lepers in the gospel whom the Lord criticized for their ingratitude after he had healed them; rather, he returned with his whole household and gave thanks to God, explaining what had happened.

This same Macarius had a hyena's den near his cell. One day the beast brought her blind cubs to him and laid them at his feet. When he realized that the animal was beseeching him concerning the cubs' blindness, he asked the Lord to grant them sight. They received it and followed their mother back to the den. Shortly afterward she emerged with the cubs, carrying in her mouth a great bunch of woolly sheepskins; she brought them to the elder as though they were a gift in return for the favor received, left them on his doorstep, and departed. But if we were to relate each of the miracles, we would fail of our planned brevity, especially since these things deserve to be told of in a book of their own.[4]

But none of them caused Lucius any shame, nor did he show any respect for the miracles. On the contrary, he ordered those fathers to be taken from their flock, or rather clandestinely seized and brought to an island in one of the marshes of Egypt, on which he had found out that there was not a single Christian, to live there deprived of any comfort and of their usual activities. The elders were thus taken by night, with only two attendants, to the island, on which there was a temple greatly revered by the inhabitants of the place. And behold, when the elders' boat touched shore there, the virgin daughter of the priest of the temple was suddenly seized by a spirit, and moving through the midst of the people began to give vent to loud shouts and shrieks which echoed to heaven, whirling about repeatedly and with shrill cries jerking her head frenziedly in every direction. And when the people gathered to watch this enormous portent, especially since it was the priest's daughter, whom they held in particular honor, she was snatched into the air and they followed her to the elders' boat. There, cast down at their feet and lying prostrate, she began to cry, "Why have you come here, O servants of God most high, to drive us from our ancient and long-held habitations? In this place we hid when we were driven out everywhere else. How is it that we have found no way to hide from you? We yield our ancient dwellings; take your peoples and lands." When she had spoken thus, the spirit of error fled at their reprimand, and the girl, restored to her senses, lay with her parents at the feet of the apostles of our time. They used this as the starting point to preach to them the faith of the Lord Jesus Christ, and brought them at once to such a complete conversion that with their own hands they immediately tore down the temple, ancient and greatly revered though it was, and lost no time in building a church; nor did they need any time to consider, since their faith had been produced not by words but by power. When this was made known in Alexandria, however, Lucius, afraid that even his own people might rightly come to hate him, seeing as he had now openly declared war not on men, but on God, ordered that they be called back secretly and returned to the desert. While this was taking place in Egypt, the flames of persecution did not die down even in other places.[5]

**11.5.** For Edessa in Mesopotamia, which is adorned with the relics of the apostle Thomas, is a city of the faithful. When the emperor saw there for himself the people who had been ejected from the churches meeting in a field, he is said to have become so angry that he struck his prefect with his fist because they had not been driven from there as well, as he had ordered. The prefect, however, although he was a pagan and had been mistreated by the emperor, was still moved by kindness to inform the citizens by secret means that he was due to go forth the next day to slaughter the people, so that they might take care not to be found in the place. And in the morning when he went forth, he made an even more fearful appearance than usual with his retinue, and a great stir, so that as few people as possible, or perhaps even no one at all, might be put in any danger. But he saw more people than usual heading for the place, running at full speed, hurrying as though fearful lest anyone should miss death. At the same time he saw a woman come bursting out of her house with such haste and speed that she took the time neither to close the door nor to cover herself properly as women should; she was pulling with her a small child and hurrying along at such a rate that she even collided with the retinue. At which, unable to restrain himself any longer, he said, "Seize that woman and bring her here." When she had been brought to him, he said, "Unhappy woman, where are you hastening with such speed?" "To the field," she said, "where the Catholic people meet." "And have you not heard," he said, "that the prefect is making his way there to kill everyone he finds?" "I have heard it and so I am hurrying, that I may be found there." "And where," he asked, "are you taking the child?" "So that it too," she replied, "may deserve to achieve martyrdom." When that mildest of men heard that, he ordered his retinue to go back, and his vehicle to turn its course to the palace, and going in he said, "Emperor, I am ready to suffer death, if you order, but the deed you command I cannot carry out." And when he had reported all that concerned the woman, he checked the emperor's madness.[6]

**11.6.** During this time the church shone with a purer light than gold in the fire of persecution. For the faith of each was tried not in words but in exiles and imprisonments, since being Catholic was not a matter of honor but of punishment, especially in Alexandria, where the faithful were not even free to bury the bodies of the dead. While Lucius was behaving thus with all arrogance and cruelty, Mavia, the queen of the Saracens, began to rock the towns and cities on the borders of Palestine and Arabia with fierce attacks, and to lay waste the neighboring provinces at the same time; she also wore down the Roman army in frequent battles, killed many, and put the rest to flight. Sued for peace, she said she would agree to it only if a monk named Moses were ordained bishop for her people. He was leading a solitary life in the desert near her territory and had achieved great fame because of his merits and the miracles and signs God worked through him. Her request, when presented to the Roman sovereign, was ordered to be carried out without delay by our officers who had fought there with such unhappy results. Moses was taken and brought to Alexandria, as was usual, to receive the priesthood. Lucius, to whom the ceremony of ordination was entrusted, was present. Moses, when he saw him, said to the officers who were there and were anxious to make haste, and to the people, "I do not think that I am worthy of such a great priesthood, but if it is judged that some part of God's providence is to be fulfilled in me, unworthy as I am, then I swear by our God, the Lord of heaven and earth, that Lucius shall not lay on me his hands, defiled and stained as they are by the blood of the saints." Lucius, seeing himself branded with so heavy a reproach in the eyes of the multitude, said, "Why, Moses, do you so easily condemn one whose faith you do not know? Or if someone has told you something different about me, listen to my creed, and believe yourself rather than others." "Lucius," he replied, "stop trying to assail even me with your delusions. I know well your creed, which God's servants condemned to the mines declare, as do the bishops driven into exile, the presbyters and deacons banished to dwellings beyond the pale of the Christian religion, and the others handed over some to the beasts and some even to fire. Can that faith be truer which is perceived by the ears than that which is seen by the eyes? I am sure that those with a correct belief in Christ do not do such things." And thus Lucius, now loaded with even more disgrace, was forced to agree that he might receive the priesthood from the bishops he had driven into exile, since the need to look to the welfare of the state was so pressing. Having received it, he both preserved the peace with that fiercest of peoples and maintained unimpaired the heritage of the Catholic faith.[7]

**II.7.** Now in Alexandria, when the foul darkness of the heresy of the murky teacher was covering the people and city, the Lord lit Didymus to be like a lamp shining with divine light. Of his life and manners we think it necessary to make brief mention, if only in passing, since he is believed to have been given by God for the glory of the church. When he was a child he was deprived of his sight even before he knew the first letters of the alphabet, but he was inflamed with an even greater desire for the knowledge of the true light; nor did he despair of gaining what he sought, since he had heard what is written in the gospel: "What is impossible for human beings is possible for God."[8] Trusting in this divine promise, he prayed to the Lord unceasingly not that he might receive sight in his eyes of flesh, but the illumination of the heart. He combined study and labor with his prayers and had recourse to continuous and uninterrupted hours of wakefulness not for reading but for listening, that what sight gave to others hearing might give to him. But when as usual sleep had overtaken the readers after their nocturnal work, Didymus, believing that the silence was not given for repose or idleness, would recall everything that he had received like a clean animal chewing its cud,[9] and would retrace in his mind and memory what he had earlier understood from the reading of the books which the others had run through, so that he seemed not so much to have heard what had been read as to have copied it out on the pages of his mind. Thus in a short time, with God as his teacher, he arrived at such expert knowledge of things divine and human that he became the master of the church school, having won the high esteem of Bishop Athanasius and the other wise men in God's church. Not only that, he was so well trained in the other disciplines, whether of dialectic or geometry, astronomy and arithmetic, that no philosopher could ever defeat or reduce him to silence by proposing any question from these arts; no sooner did he hear his answers than he was convinced that he was an expert in the discipline in question. A number of people with the help of stenographers took down what he said, his debates with others, and his replies to the issues raised, all of which is still held in great admiration. We, however, who were both in some sense disciples of his when he spoke in person, and who also read what he said as taken down by a good number of people, perceived a far greater grace and something divine and above human speech which sounded rather in those words which came from his mouth. The blessed Antony too, when he was on his way down to Alexandria from the Thebaid to bear witness against the Arians with the faith of Athanasius, consoled him with these marvelous words: "Do not be troubled, Didymus, by the deprivation of your physical eyes, for what you lack are those eyes which mice, flies, and lizards have; rejoice rather that you have the eyes which angels have, by which God is seen, and through which a great light of knowledge is being lit for you."[10]

11.8. Egypt was flourishing at that time not only with men steeped in Christian learning, but also with those who dwelt throughout the great desert and worked the signs and wonders of apostles in simplicity of life and sincerity of heart. Those of them whom at that time we ourselves saw and by whose hands it was granted us to be blessed are the following: Macarius of the upper desert, another Macarius of the lower, Isidore in Scete, Pambo in Cellulae, Moses and Benjamin in Nitria, Ischyrion, Elias, and Paul in Apeliotes, another Paul in Foci(?), and Poemen and Joseph in Pispir, which was called Antony's mountain. We learned as well from reliable report that a great many other men of this sort dwelt in Egypt, so that the apostle's statement was truly fulfilled: where sin abounded, grace has abounded far more.[11] Mesopotamia also at this same time had noble men who excelled in this same way of life. Some of them we saw with our own eyes in Edessa and Carrhae, while we heard about even more of them.[12]

11.9. But Cappadocia was no less fertile than either of these; if anything, it gave us an even richer crop in Gregory and Basil. It therefore bore a generous harvest of many saints, produced a luxurious vineyard of religious folk, and brought forth a young olive sprout for the Lord. But it was they especially who, like two sons of plenty standing on the right and left of the lampstand,[13] shone forth like two luminaries in the sky, so that I think it would be good to put down a little more about them. Both were of noble families, both studied in Athens where they were fellow students, and both upon leaving the lecture hall were sought after as rhetoricians. But as wonderfully as Basil practiced this art, Gregory still more wonderfully disdained it. And since he had given himself wholly to God's service, he presumed upon his companion's

love to such an extent that he removed Basil from the professor's chair
which he was occupying and forced him to accompany him to a monastery, where for thirteen years, they say, having put aside all the writings of the worldly pagans, they gave their attention solely to the books
of holy scripture, the understanding of which they did not presume to
derive from themselves, but from the writings and authority of those
of old who were themselves known to have received the rule of understanding from apostolic tradition. They sought the treasures of wisdom and knowledge hidden in these vessels of clay by examining their
commentaries on the prophets in particular.[14]

Now when they had learned as much as they needed, divine providence called them to instruct the people; each was drawn by a different route to the same task. Basil went round the cities and countryside
of Pontus and began by his words to rouse that province from its tor-
por and lack of concern for our hope for the future, kindling it by his
preaching, and to banish the insensitivity resulting from long negli-
gence; he compelled it to put away its concern for vain and worldly
things and to give its attention to him. He taught the people to assemble, to build monasteries, to give time to psalms, hymns, and
prayers, to take care of the poor and furnish them with proper hous-
ing and the necessities of life, to establish the way of life of virgins,
and to make the life of modesty and chastity desirable to almost everyone. In a short time the appearance of the whole province was so trans-
formed that a generous crop and a luxuriant vineyard had sprung into
view in what had been a dry and barren field.[15]

Gregory, for his part, would not allow good seed to lie on top of
thorns or be scattered among rocks,[16] but he cultivated the good earth
of his heart with unremitting diligence and continuous discipline,
achieving much greater results in himself than Basil did in others. While
Basil had charge of receiving what those who renounced the world laid
at his feet and of dividing it according to the needs of each, Gregory,
content with the words of scripture about having nothing and pos-
sessing everything,[17] longed only for the riches of wisdom and clung
to them with great desire. While Basil taught the multitude to assemble
together and to have concern for one another's needs, Gregory by his
own example, an eloquent book, preached to everyone the apostolic
message: "I wish you to be without concern," and "The Lord is near;

do not be concerned," but as servants of Christ be concerned with one thing only: the time of the Lord's return from the wedding.[18] Basil showed his compassion in commiserating with the fallen and calling them back from sin; Gregory by the gift of his divine eloquence removed the temptations to sin and did not allow those to fall who once injured could be made to stand again only with difficulty. Basil was pure in faith, Gregory freer in preaching. Basil was humble in God's sight, Gregory was so in the people's view as well. Basil conquered the arrogant by disdain, Gregory by reason. Thus it was that a different grace was active in each of them to achieve one work of perfection.

Basil, then, who not long after was bishop of Caesarea in Cappadocia, when he was about to be banished by Valens for the faith, was hailed into the prefect's court and subjected to the terrors and grievous threats customary to that power, and told that unless he obeyed the emperor's orders he might expect instant death. He is said to have replied with calm fearlessness to the prefect who was threatening him, "I wish I had some worthy gift to offer to him who would give Basil early release from this knotted bag." And when he was given the intervening night to consider, he is reported to have replied once more, "I will be tomorrow who I am now, and you will certainly be no different." And behold, that night the emperor's wife was racked with pain as though under torture, while their only son died: in retribution, it is believed, for his father's impiety. Thus there came messengers before daybreak to ask Basil to intercede for them in prayer, lest they should also die, and indeed with far more justice. That is how it came about that when Valens drove out all the Catholics, Basil stayed in the church for the rest of his life without compromising the bond of communion.[19]

Now Gregory, who had succeeded his father as bishop in the town of Nazianzus, bore steadfastly the disturbances of the heretics. But when peace was restored he did not refuse the plea to come to Constantinople to instruct the church. There in a short time he did so much to cure the people of the chronic illness of heresy that it seemed to them that they were becoming Christians and seeing the new light of truth for the first time, now that the teacher of religion was instructing them; much as he did this by his words, yet he taught them still more by his example, and it seemed that he told his disciples to do nothing which he had not done first. But envy followed upon glory, and there were some who began to resist him and to suggest baseless arguments why he should return to his own place and another be ordained bishop. This he heard being whispered and murmured only, but he brought out into the open what nobody had dared tell him: "Let there not be any dissension among God's priests on my account," he said. "If this storm has arisen because of me, take me away and throw me into the sea, and let your agitation cease." He then returned to his church and spent the rest of his life there. Because he was advanced in age and physically weak, he designated his own successor, who could take charge of the church and allow him the leisure of his infirmity and old age.[20]

We still have as well some wonderful testimonials to the genius of both men in the form of sermons which they delivered *ex tempore* in the churches. Of these we have translated into Latin about ten of the short discourses of each of them, as well as the monastic rules of Basil, hoping if possible and with God's help to translate more of their works. Basil also had two brothers, Gregory and Peter, of whom the first so rivaled his brother in doctrinal exposition and the second in works of faith, that either was simply another Basil or Gregory. We also still have some short, excellent works of the younger Gregory. But enough about them.[21]

In the West, meanwhile, Valentinian, his religious faith untarnished, was ruling the state with the vigilance traditional to Roman government.

**II.IO.** Damasus succeeded Liberius in the priesthood in the city of Rome. Ursinus, a deacon of this church, unable to accept his being preferred to himself, became so unhinged that with the aid of some naive, inexperienced bishop, whom he persuaded, and a riotous and unruly gang which he got together, he forced through his ordination as bishop in the Basilica of Sicininus, overturning in his path law, order, and tradition. This caused such a riot, or rather such battles between the people siding with the two men, that the places of prayer ran with human blood. The affair resulted in such ill will toward a good and innocent priest, due to the conduct of the prefect Maximinus, that misguided man, that the case led even to the torture of clerics. But God, the protector of the innocent, came to the rescue, and punishment reverted upon the heads of those who had plotted treachery.[22]

**11.11.** In Milan meanwhile Auxentius, the bishop of the heretics, died, and the people were divided into two parties with different loyalties. The disagreement and strife were so serious and dangerous that they threatened the very city with speedy disaster, should either side not get what it wanted, since both desired something different. Ambrose was then governor of the province. When he saw the city on the brink of destruction, he immediately entered the church, as his office and the place required, in order to calm the riotous crowd. While engaged there in a lengthy speech about law and public order for the sake of peace and tranquillity, there suddenly arose from the people fighting and quarreling with each other a single voice which shouted that it would have Ambrose as bishop; they cried that he should be baptized forthwith, for he was a catechumen, and given to them as bishop, nor could there be one people and one faith otherwise, unless Ambrose was given to them as priest. While he struggled and resisted strongly against this, the people's wish was reported to the emperor, who ordered it to be fulfilled with all speed. For, he said, it was thanks to God that this sudden conversion had recalled the diverse religious attitudes and discordant views of the people to a single viewpoint and attitude. Yielding to God's grace, Ambrose received the sacred initiation and the priesthood without delay.[23]

**11.12.** During this time Valentinian, who had made his way from Gaul to Illyricum to fight the Sarmatians, was struck down by sudden illness there when the war had just begun; he left as heirs to the empire his sons the Augustus Gratian and Valentinian, who was quite young and had not yet received the imperial tokens. But pressure from those who were trying to usurp power as though the government were vacant forced him to assume the purple even though his brother was absent; Probus, then prefect, faithfully carried the matter out.[24]

**11.13.** In the Eastern empire meanwhile the Goths, driven from their homes, spread throughout the provinces of Thrace and began a savage destruction of cities and countryside with their weapons. Then Valens did begin to redirect his military efforts away from the churches and toward the enemy, and with belated regret ordered bishops and priests to be recalled from exile and monks to be released from the mines. But he was surrounded by the enemy on an estate to which he had fled in fear from battle, and paid the price for his impiety by being burned to ashes, having reigned his first year with his brother and afterward for fourteen years with his brothers' sons as well. This battle was the beginning of evil times for the Roman empire from then on.[25] Gratian, then, with his very young brother, succeeded to the Eastern empire as well after his uncle's death. In piety and religious fervor he excelled almost all the previous rulers. He was vigorous in armed combat, physically quick, and intelligent, but his youthful bois-terousness went almost too far, and he was too modest for the good of the state.

II.I4. Seeing that it would be useful to have a man of mature age to share the many cares of government, and since, as holy scripture teaches, two are better than one, he associated Theodosius with himself, giv-ing him charge of the East and retaining the West for his brother and himself. After many pious and brave deeds, however, he was killed in Lyons by Maximus, the usurper from Britain, who acted through the officer Andragathius: an act of treachery by his own people rather than an enemy stroke.[26]

II.I5. In Italy Valentinian, terrified by his brother's murder and in dread of the enemy, gladly pretended to embrace the peace which Maximus pretended to offer. Meanwhile his mother Justina, a disciple of the Arian sect, boldly uncorked for her gullible son the poisons of her impiety which she had kept hidden while her husband was alive. Thus while residing in Milan she upset the churches and threatened the priests with deposition and exile unless they reinstated the decrees of the Council of Ariminum by which the faith of the fathers had been violated. In this war she assailed Ambrose, the wall of the church and its stoutest tower, harassing him with threats, terrors, and every kind of attack as she sought a first opening into the church she wanted to conquer. But while she fought armed with the spirit of Jezebel, Ambrose stood firm, filled with the power and grace of Elijah. She went about the churches chattering noisily and trying to rouse and kindle discord among the people, but when she failed, she regarded herself as having been wronged, and complained to her son. The youth, indignant at the tale of outrage concocted by his mother, sent a band of armed men to the church with orders to smash the doors, attack the sanctuary, drag out the priest, and send him into exile forthwith. But the steadfastness of the faithful was such that they would rather have lost their lives than their bishop.[27]

**11.16.** Meanwhile imperial decrees contrary to the faith of the fathers were sent for drafting to Benivolus, then *magister memoriae*. But this faith had been held in holy awe by him since infancy, and he said that he could not make impious statements and speak against God. Then, lest the empress's plans be foiled, he was promised advancement if he did as he had been told. But he desired to advance in faith rather than in honors, and so he said, "Why do you promise me higher rank in return for impiety? Take away the one I have; only let my conscience remain clear about the faith." Saying this he threw down his belt at the feet of those who were ordering the impious deed.[28]

Ambrose for his part did not ward off the empress's fury with hand or weapon, but with fasts and unceasing vigils at the foot of the altar set himself to win God by his prayers to his and the church's cause. And when Justina had spent a good while contriving these schemes and methods of attack, to no avail, Maximus, eager to rid himself of the stigma of usurpation and to show himself a legitimate ruler, declared in a letter he sent that what she was attempting was impious and that the faith of God was being attacked and the laws of the Catholic Church destroyed; at the same time he began to move toward Italy. Justina, upon learning this, under pressure from both her enemy and her bad conscience, took flight with her son and was the first to undergo the exile she had planned for God's priests.[29]

**11.17.** Theodosius, however, kept faith both with the realm and with the memory of Gratian's good character and deeds; arriving with all the forces of the East, he avenged his just blood and, once the usurpation had been put down, restored to Valentinian both the Catholic faith violated by his irreligious mother, who died at this time, and the realm. And after he had ridden into Rome in a glorious triumph, he returned to his own territory.[30]

**II.18.** During this time the pious sovereign was vilely besmirched by the demon's cunning. It happened when a military officer was attacked during a riot in Thessalonica and killed by the angry people. Furious at the atrocity when the unexpected news was announced, he ordered the people to be invited to a circus, to be surrounded suddenly by soldiers, and to be cut down by the sword indiscriminately, anyone who was there, and thus to satisfy not justice but anger. When he was reproved for this by the priests of Italy, he admitted the crime, acknowledged his sin with tears, did public penance in the sight of the whole church and, putting aside the imperial pomp, patiently completed the time prescribed him for it. To all of this he added something wonderful: he made it a law from then on that the punitive decrees of sovereigns should not be executed until thirty days had elapsed, in order not to lose the opportunity for leniency, or even, should circumstances suggest, for reconsideration.[31]

**II.19.** He returned therefore to the East, and there showed the greatest care and eagerness, as he had since the beginning of his reign, in driving out the heretics and handing over the churches to the Catholics. He exercised such moderation in doing so that, rejecting all motives of revenge, he took measures to restore the churches to the Catholics only insofar as the true faith could make progress once the obstacle to its being preached had been removed. He behaved unpretentiously toward the priests of God, while to all others he showed his kingly spirit in his faith, piety, and generosity. He was easy to approach, showing no imperial disdain in speaking to commoners. Through his exhortation and generosity churches in many places were amply furnished and magnificently built. He gave much to those who asked, but frequently offered yet more. Idolatry, which following upon Constantine's initiative had begun to be neglected and demolished, collapsed during his reign. For these reasons he was so dear to God that divine Providence granted him a special favor: it filled with the prophetic spirit a monk named John in the Thebaid, so that by his counsel and replies he could learn whether it would be better to remain at peace or go to war.[32]

**II.20.** Before this, meanwhile, Bishop Apollinaris of Laodicea in Syria, a man who was quite well educated but who had a great weakness for argument and enjoyed going against whatever anyone said, such was his unfortunate talent for flaunting his intelligence, produced from his contentiousness a heresy according to which the Lord assumed only a body, but not a soul as well, in the Incarnation. Pressed on this point by clear passages in the gospel where the Lord and Savior himself states that he has a soul and lays it down when he wants and takes it up again, and where he says that it is troubled and saddened even unto death,[33] he later changed his position, and lest he appear quite defeated, said that while he did have a soul, it did not have the part by which it is rational, but only that by which it vivifies the body. The Word of God himself, he states, supplied for the rational part. This teaching was first rejected in the city of Rome by Damasus and Bishop Peter of Alexandria in council assembled in the following terms: they ruled that whoever said that the Son of God, who just as he was truly God so also was truly a human being, lacked anything human or divine, should be considered alien to the church. This judgment was ratified in Alexandria and Constantinople by conciliar decree, and from then on the Apollinarians, turning aside from the church, have maintained an episcopate for their sect together with their own doctrines and churches.[34]

**11.21.** In the city of Rome, then, Siricius received the priesthood after Damasus. As for Alexandria, when Peter died Timothy succeeded him and then Theophilus, while in Jerusalem John followed Cyril. When Meletius died Flavian took his place in Antioch. Paulinus, however, who had always remained in communion with the Catholics, was still alive, and this caused a good many quarrels and disputes there on many occasions, nor did the most determined efforts on either side, with the very elements of earth and sea worn out in the struggle, ever succeed in producing any measure of peace, since there no longer seemed to be any disagreement about doctrine. The same was true in Tyre, where Diodore, one of the long-standing Catholics proven by perseverance in trial, was made bishop by the confessors with Athanasius's approval; but his mildness was looked down upon and someone else was ordained by Meletius's party. In many other Eastern cities as well the priests' quarrels resulted in confusion of this sort. In Constantinople, in fact, Nectarius went

from the position of urban praetor to catechumen, and shortly thereafter received baptism and the priesthood.[35]

**II.22.** In Alexandria meanwhile fresh disturbances broke out against
the church in opposition to the religious faith of the times; the occasion was as follows. There was an ancient basilica built for public use,
but quite untended, which the emperor Constantius was said to have
donated to the bishops of his heretical faith, and which long neglect
had so reduced that only the walls were still sound. The bishop who
had charge of the church at that time decided to ask the emperor for
it so that the growth of the houses of prayer might keep pace with the
growing number of the faithful. He received it and was setting about
restoring it when some hidden grottoes and underground chambers
were discovered on the site which smacked more of lawlessness and
crimes than of religious services. The pagans therefore, when they saw
the dens of their iniquity and caverns of sin being uncovered, could
not bear to have exposed this evil which long ages had covered and
darkness had concealed, but began all of them, as though they had
drunk the serpents' cup,[36] to behave violently and to give vent to their
fury in public. Nor was it just their usual noisy demonstrations; they
used weapons, battling up and down the streets so that the two sides
were at open war. Our side far outweighed the other in numbers and
strength, but was less savage due to the mild character of our religion.
As a result many of ours were wounded in the repeated conflicts, and
some were even killed. Then they took refuge in a [the?] temple,[37]
using it as a stronghold and taking with them many Christians whom
they had captured. These they forced to offer sacrifice on the altars
where fire was kindled; those who refused they put to death with new
and refined tortures, fastening some to gibbets and breaking the legs
of others and pitching them into the caverns which a careworn antiquity had built to receive the blood of sacrifices and the other impuri-
ties of the temple.

They carried on in this way day after day, first fearfully and then
with boldness and desperation, living shut up within the temple on
plunder and booty. Finally, setting their sights on the lives of the citizens, they chose one Olympus, a philosopher in name and garb only,

as leader of their criminal and impudent band, so that with him as standard-bearer they might defend their stronghold and maintain the usurpation. But when those charged with maintaining the laws of Rome and giving judgment learned what had happened, they rushed to the temple in terrified agitation and asked the reasons for this rash behavior and the meaning of the riot in which the blood of citizens had been so wickedly spilled before the altars. But they barricaded the entrance and with confused and discordant voices replied with shouts rather than explanations for what they had done. Messages however were sent to them to remind them of the power of the Roman government, of the legal penalties, and of the normal consequences of behavior of the sort, and since the place was so fortified that nothing could be done against those attempting such madness except by drastic action, the matter was reported to the emperor. Being more inclined to correct than to destroy the errant because of his great clemency, he wrote back that satisfaction was not to be sought for those whom their blood shed before the altars had made martyrs and the glory of whose merits had overcome the pain of their death, but that otherwise the cause of the evils and the roots of the discord which had taken up the defense of the idols should be eliminated, so that once these were done away with, the reason for the conflict might also disappear. Now when this letter arrived and both peoples met together at the temple following a sort of short-term truce, no sooner had the first page been read out, the introduction to which criticized the vain superstition of the pagans, than a great shout was raised by our people, while shock and fear assailed the pagans, each of whom sought to hide somewhere, to find alleys through which to flee, or to slip unnoticed among our people. Thus all who were there realized that God's presence giving courage to his people had put to flight the demon's fury which had earlier raged among the pagans.[38]

11.23. I suppose that everyone has heard of the temple of Serapis in Alexandria, and that many are also familiar with it. The site was elevated, not naturally but artificially, to a height of a hundred or more steps, its enormous rectangular premises extending in every direction. All the rooms up to the floor on top were vaulted, and being furnished with ceiling lights and concealed inner chambers separate from one another, were used for various services and secret functions. On the upper level, furthermore, the outermost structures in the whole circumference provided space for halls and shrines and for lofty apartments which normally housed either the temple staff or those called *hagneuontes*, meaning those who keep themselves pure. Behind these in turn were porticoes arranged in rectangles which ran around the whole circumference on the inside. In the middle of the entire area rose the sanctuary with priceless columns, the exterior fashioned of marble, spacious and magnificent to behold. In it there was a statue of Serapis so large that its right hand touched one wall and its left the other; this monster is said to have been made of every kind of metal and wood. The interior walls of the shrine were believed to have been covered with plates of gold overlaid with silver and then bronze, the last as a protection for the more precious metals.[39]

There were also some things cunningly devised to excite the amazement and wonder of those who saw them. There was a tiny window so orientated toward the direction of sunrise that on the day appointed for the statue of the sun to be carried in to greet Serapis, careful observation of the seasons had ensured that as the statue was entering, a ray of sunlight coming through this window would light up the mouth and lips of Serapis, so that to the people looking on it would seem as though the sun was greeting Serapis with a kiss.

There was another like trick. Magnets, it is said, have the power to pull and draw iron to themselves. The image of the sun had been made by its artisan of the finest sort of iron with this in view: that a magnet, which, as we said, naturally attracts iron, and which was set in the ceiling panels, might by natural force draw the iron to itself when the statue was placed just so directly beneath it, the statue appearing to the people to rise and hang in the air. And lest it unexpectedly fall and betray the trick, the servants of the deception would say, "The sun has arisen so that, bidding Serapis farewell, it may depart for its own place." There were many other things as well built on the site by those of old for the purpose of deception which it would take too long to detail.[40]

Now as we started to say, when the letter had been read our people were ready to overthrow the author of [the] error, but a rumor had been spread by the pagans that if a human hand touched the statue, the earth would split open on the spot and crumble into the abyss, while the sky would crash down at once. This gave the people pause for a moment, until one of the soldiers, armed with faith rather than weapons, seized a double-headed axe, drew himself up, and struck the old fraud on the jaw with all his might. A roar went up from both sides, but the sky did not fall, nor did the earth collapse. Thus with repeated strokes he felled the smoke-grimed deity of rotten wood, which upon being thrown down burned as easily as dry wood when it was kindled. After this the head was wrenched from the neck, the bushel having been taken down, and dragged off; then the feet and other members were chopped off with axes and dragged apart with ropes attached, and piece by piece, each in a different place, the decrepit dotard was burned to ashes before the eyes of the Alexandria which had worshiped him. Last of all the torso which was left was put to the torch in the amphitheater, and that was the end of the vain superstition and ancient error of Serapis.[41]

The pagans have different views about his origin. Some regard him as Jupiter, the bushel placed upon his head showing either that he governs all things with moderation and restraint or that he bestows life on mortals through the bounty of harvests. Others regard him as the power of the Nile River, by whose richness and fertility Egypt is fed. There are some who think the statue was made in honor of our Joseph because of the distribution of grain by which he aided the Egyptians in the time of famine. Still others claim to have found in Greek histories of old that a certain Apis, the head of a house or a king located in Memphis in Egypt, provided ample food from his own store to the citizens when the grain ran out in Alexandria during a famine. When he died, they founded a temple in his honor in Memphis in which a bull, the symbol of the ideal farmer, is fed; it has certain markings on its hide and is called "Apis" after him. As for the *soros* or coffin in which his body lay, they brought it down to Alexandria and by putting together *soros* and *Apis* they at first called him "Sorapis," but this was later corrupted to "Serapis." God knows what truth if any there is in all this. But let us return to the subject.[42]

II.24. Once the very pinnacle of idolatry had been thrown down, all of the idols, or one should rather say monsters, throughout Alexandria were pilloried by a like destruction and similar disgrace through the efforts of its most vigilant priest. The mind shudders to speak of the snares laid by the demons for wretched mortals, the corpses, the crimes uncovered in what they call "shrines," the number of decapitated babies' heads found in gilded urns, the number of pictures of excruciating deaths of poor wretches. When these were brought to light and displayed to public view, even though their very confusion and shame scattered the pagans, still those who could bear to remain were amazed at how they had been enmeshed for so many centuries in such vile and shameful deceptions. Hence many of them, having condemned this error and realized its wickedness, embraced the faith of Christ and the true religion. To pass over the other enormities committed elsewhere, the children murdered and the virgins disemboweled for extispicy, I shall record only the one which was brought to everyone's notice as having been committed in the temple of Saturn; from it one may get some idea of the others not mentioned.[43]

**11.25.** They had a priest of Saturn named Tyrannus. He used to tell whichever of the nobles and leading men who worshiped in the temple and whose wives attracted his lust that Saturn had told him (he pretended that the deity had spoken in answer) that his wife was to spend the night in the temple. The one so informed, overjoyed that the deity had deigned to summon his wife, would send her to the temple elegantly adorned, and laden with offerings as well, lest she be spurned for coming empty-handed. The wife was locked inside in full view of everyone, and Tyrannus, once the doors were shut and the keys handed over, would depart. Then when silence had fallen he would make his way through hidden underground passages and creep right into the very statue of Saturn, entering through wide-open cavities—for the statue had been hollowed out in the back and was fastened snugly to the wall—and while the lamps were burning within the shrine a voice from the hollow bronze statue would speak suddenly to the woman rapt in prayer, so that the unfortunate woman would tremble for fear and joy, thinking that she had been found worthy to be addressed by this great deity. After the foul deity had spoken to her in whatever terms he chose to increase her fear or arouse her lust, the wicks would be snuffed by some device and suddenly all the lamps would go out. Then, descending upon the poor woman in her amazement and confusion, he would commit with her the adultery disguised by his unholy language. When he had carried on in this way for quite some time with all the wives of those wretches, it happened that one of the women, whose modesty shrank from this misdeed, listened closely, recognized Tyrannus's voice, returned home, and reported the crime to her husband. Furious at the wrong done to his wife, and even more to himself, he had Tyrannus charged and handed over to torture. With his conviction and confession and his secret misdeeds brought to light, shame and disgrace flooded all the houses of the pagans with the discovery of adulterous mothers, doubtful fathers, and illegitimate children. When all this was revealed and publicized, there was a rush to extirpate the idols and shrines, and along with them the crimes as well.[44]

11.26. As for Canopus, who could list the enormities connected with its cult? There was what amounted to a public school of magic there under the guise of the study of the priestly writing, for so they call the ancient writing of the Egyptians. The pagans revered the place as a source and origin of [the] demons to such an extent that its popularity was far greater than that of Alexandria. Now it will not be out of place to explain briefly how the tradition accounts for the error connected with this monster as well. They say that once upon a time the Chaldaeans made a tour carrying with them their god, fire, and held a contest with the gods of all the provinces, the winner of which should be regarded by all as god. The gods of all the other provinces were of bronze or gold or silver or wood or stone or of whatever material is of course spoiled by fire. And thus fire prevailed everywhere. When the priest of Canopus heard this, he thought of a clever plan. Earthenware water pots are commonly manufactured in Egypt which are densely stippled all over with tiny holes, so that when cloudy water trickles through them the sediment is strained out and it becomes purer. He took one, stopped up the holes with wax, painted it various colors, filled it with water, set it up as a god, and on its top carefully fitted the head cut off of an old statue said to have been that of Menelaus's helmsman. Then when the Chaldaeans arrived, the contest was held, and when fire was kindled around the water pot, the wax stopping the holes melted, the fire was quenched by the perspiring pot, and the priest's craft gave the victory to Canopus over the Chaldaeans. Hence the statue itself of Canopus was in the form of a water pot, with tiny feet, an almost comically squat neck, bulging stomach, and an equally rounded back, and on account of this tradition was worshiped as an all-conquering god. But whatever he may once have done to the Chaldaeans, now with the arrival of the priest of God, Theophilus, neither his perspiration nor his wax-covered tricks were of any avail; everything was destroyed and razed to the ground.[45]

**II.27.** But nothing was done which resulted in the place becoming deserted. The dens of iniquity and age-worn burial grounds were demolished, and lofty churches, temples of the true God, were put up. For on the site of Serapis's tomb the unholy sanctuaries were leveled, and on the one side there rose a martyr's shrine, on the other a church. I think it would be worthwhile to explain why the martyr's shrine was built.[46]

**II.28.** In Julian's time the ferocity of the pagans sprang forth in all its savagery, as though the reins had gone slack. Thus it happened that in Sebaste, a city of Palestine, they frenziedly attacked the tomb of John the Baptist with murderous hands and set about scattering the bones, gathering them again, burning them, mixing the holy ashes with dust, and scattering them throughout the fields and countryside. But by God's providence it happened that some men from Jerusalem, from the monastery of Philip, the man of God, arrived there at the same time in order to pray. When they saw the enormity being perpetrated by human hands at the service of bestial spirits, they mixed with those gathering the bones for burning, since they considered dying preferable to being polluted by such a sin, carefully and reverently collected them, as far as they could in the circumstances, then slipped away from the others, to their amazement or fury, and brought the sacred relics to the pious father Philip. He in turn, thinking it beyond him to guard such a treasure by his own vigilance, sent the relics of this spotless victim to Athanasius, then supreme pontiff, in the care of his deacon Julian, who later became bishop of Parentium. Athanasius received them and closed them up within a hollowed-out place in the sacristy wall in the presence of a few witnesses, preserving them in prophetic spirit for the benefit of the next generation, so that now that the remnants of idolatry had been thrown down flat, golden roofs might rise for them on temples once unholy.[47]

But after the death of Serapis, who had never been alive, what temples of any other demon could remain standing? It would hardly be enough to say that all the deserted shrines in Alexandria, of whatever demon, came down almost column by column. In fact, in all the cities of Egypt, the settlements, the villages, the countryside everywhere, the riverbanks, even the desert, wherever shrines, or rather graveyards, could be found, the persistence of the several bishops resulted in their being wrecked and razed to the ground, so that the countryside, which had wrongly been given over to the demons, was restored to agriculture.[48]

**11.29.** Another thing was done in Alexandria: the busts of Serapis, which had been in every house in the walls, the entrances, the doorposts, and even the windows, were so cut and filed away that not even a trace or mention of him or any other demon remained anywhere. In their place everyone painted the sign of the Lord's cross on doorposts, entrances, windows, walls, and columns. It is said that when the pagans who were left saw this, they were reminded of an important tradition which had come down to them from of old. The Egyptians are said to have this our sign of the Lord's cross among the characters which they call "hieratic," or priestly, as one of the letters making up their script. They state that the meaning of this character or noun is "the life to come." Those then who were coming over to the faith out of astonishment at what was happening said that it had been handed down to them from of old that the things now worshiped would remain until they saw that the sign had come in which was life. Hence it was the temple priests and ministers who came over to the faith rather than those who enjoyed the tricks of error and devices of deceit.[49]

**11.30.** Now it was the custom in Egypt to bring the gauge of the rising Nile River to the temple of Serapis, as being the one who caused the increase of water and the flooding; so when his statue was overthrown and burned, everyone of course unanimously declared that Serapis, mindful of this injury, would never again bestow the waters in their usual abundance. But so that God could show that it was he who ordered the waters of the river to rise in season, and not Serapis, who after all was much younger than the Nile, there began then such a succession of floods as never before recorded. And thus the practice began of bringing that very measuring rod, or water gauge, which they call a *pêchys*, to the Lord of waters in the church. When these events were reported to the pious sovereign, he is said to have stretched out his arms to heaven and exclaimed with great joy, "I thank you, Christ, that this age-old error has been demolished without harm to that great city."[50]

**II.31.** The life of Valentinian, meanwhile, who had been governing the country in the West with all the enthusiasm of one of his age, was brought to an end by a noose for reasons still unknown. They asserted that it was due to a plot by his officer Arbogast, a view commonly held by the people. Others said that the officer was innocent of the crime, but had been the reason why the youth had gotten so angry that he was driven to the deed, namely because he had not allowed him completely free rein in governing since he was not yet of age. Several priests, however, who undertook an embassy of peace from the one created [emperor] afterward, testified in Theodosius's presence that the officer was innocent of the crime.[51]

**II.32.** Theodosius was aroused all the same and prepared to take up arms in revenge against Eugenius, who had succeeded the one who had died. But first he sought God's will through John, the monk we mentioned earlier. He was the one who had foretold to him the prior bloodless victory over Maximus; this time he promised another victory, but not without great bloodshed on both sides.[52]

**II.33.** He made ready then for war by arming himself not so much with weapons as with fasts and prayers; guarded not so much by the night watch as by nightly vigils in prayer, he would go around all the places of prayer with the priests and people, lie prostrate in sackcloth before the reliquaries of the martyrs and apostles, and implore assistance through the faithful intercession of the saints. But the pagans, who are always reviving their errors with new ones, renewed the sacrifices and bloodied Rome with horrid victims, examined sheep guts and from the divination of entrails proclaimed that victory for Eugenius was assured. Flavian, who was then prefect, engaged in this in a spirit of deep superstition and great fervor, and it was owing to his statements that they assumed that Eugenius's victory was assured, since he had a great reputation for being wise. But when Theodosius, confident in the assistance provided by the true religion, began to force the Alpine passes, the first to flee were the demons, fearfully aware of how deceitfully they had received the many victims offered to them in vain. Next were those who taught and professed these errors, especially Flavian, who was weighted with shame more than guilt. While he could have escaped, being a man of such high culture, he considered that he deserved death more justly for having erred than for any crime.[53]

The others mustered their forces and, having set ambushes at the top of the passes, they themselves waited to give battle on the downward slope of the mountain. But when contact was made with those in front and they surrendered on the spot to the legitimate sovereign, a desperate combat ensued with the others trapped deep in the gorges. For a while the outcome was in doubt; the barbarian auxiliaries were being routed and put to flight before the enemy. But this took place not so that Theodosius might be conquered, but so that he might not appear to have conquered with the help of barbarians. From his place high upon a rock, where he could observe and be observed by both armies, he saw his forces in retreat, and throwing down his weapons he turned to his accustomed source of help, prostrating himself before God. "Almighty God," he prayed, "You know that it was in the name of Christ Your Son that I undertook this war in order to exact what I consider just retribution. If this is not so, then punish me, but if I have come here in a just cause and trusting in you, then stretch out your right hand to those who are yours, lest the gentiles say: Where is their God?"[54]

The officers who were with him, certain that the prayer of the pious sovereign had been accepted by God, drew fresh courage for battle. Most notable was Bacurius, a man so outstanding in faith, piety, and strength of mind and body that he merited to serve on Theodosius's staff. He slew those he came up against on all sides with spear, arrows, and sword, pierced the thickly serried ranks of the enemy, and having broken their line made his way to the usurper himself through thousands of fleeing men and scattered heaps of corpses.

Now the impious may find this hard to believe, but it is established that following the prayer which the emperor said to God, a wind of such violence arose that it turned the enemy shafts back upon those who had launched them. The wind continued to blow with such force that all the enemy missiles were to no avail, and the adversaries' spirit was broken, or rather frustrated by Heaven despite the courageous efforts of General Arbogast, who strove in vain against God. And so Eugenius was led to Theodosius's feet with his hands tied behind him, and there ended his life and the battle. Then indeed more glory accrued to the devout sovereign's victory from the failed expectations of the pagans than from the death of the usurper, the pagans whose empty hopes and false prophecies meant that the punishment of those among them who died was less grievous than the shame of those who survived.[55]

**11.34.** Afterward the emperor, foreseeing what was to come and anxious to put the affairs of the state in order, sent at once to the East, where he had left his children in safe hands when he set out for war. He bade the Augustus Arcadius to keep the realm which had long since been handed over to him there. Honorius he invested with equal rank and ordered him to hasten to the empire of the West. When he had welcomed him with fatherly kisses and embraces and handed over to him the government of the Western realm, he himself went on to a better place to receive his reward with the most religious sovereigns, having guided the Roman empire successfully for seventeen years.[56]

### NOTES TO BOOK II

1. Jovian succeeded Julian on June 27, 363. The words "contraque omnem spem . . . subito emissos a barbaris oratores adesse vident pacemque deposcere" remind one of Ammianus Marcellinus 25.7.5: "Persae praeter sperata priores super fundanda pace oratores . . . mittunt." For Ammianus, however, the Persians' kindness was only feigned: "Condiciones autem ferebant difficiles et perplexas, fingentes humanorum respectu reliquias exercitus redire sinere clementissimum regem" (25.7.6). Jovian was in a hurry to return to Roman soil, though, because Julian was thought to have named his relative Procopius

to succeed him before he opened the campaign (Ammianus 25.3.2, 25.7.10), and he wanted to be back before Procopius could learn of Julian's death. He therefore agreed to what was regarded as a disgraceful surrender of territory and alliances in return for a thirty-year peace treaty (25.7.11–14). Cf. Soc. 3.22.1–8; Soz. 6.3.1–2; Theodoret 4.1.1–4.2.3; Zosimus 3.30–34; Eutropius 10.17.

Athanasius sailed from Egypt on September 6, 363, to meet Jovian even before the latter reached Antioch. Jovian's letter to him prefaces Athan. *Ep.* 56, which contains an exposition of the Creed of Nicaea. Despite what Rufinus says, there is no reason to think Jovian sent for him, although the emperor's letter compliments him for his courage and respectfully allows him to return to his church.

Athanasius was only one of a crowd of church leaders and other interested parties who hastened to seek Jovian out while he was still on the homeward march; those among them who tried to oppose Athanasius were rebuffed (appendix to *Ep.* 56). Jovian, while he rescinded Julian's orders banishing Athanasius, restoring state support of pagan worship (Athan. *Hist. Aceph.* 12), and canceling the grain allowance to the churches (Theodoret 4.4), refused to take sides in the controversies among his fellow Christians. He simply made it clear that he esteemed Meletius of Antioch no less than Athanasius, and many of their colleagues soon found it convenient to publish a pro-Nicene declaration (Soc. 3.25). This happy result of Jovian's policy of benign neglect encouraged stories that he had officially established the Creed of Nicaea (Theodoret 4.2.3) and may also be behind Rufinus's claim that he received a church policy ("ecclesiarum disponendarum modus") from Athanasius. Cf. also Philostorgius 8.5–6.

Jovian died in Dadastana on February 17, 364. Both the exact location of the place (in Bithynia?) and the cause of his death are uncertain; cf. Ammianus 25.10.12–13; Paschoud 2.238.

2. The "hundredfold" refers to Mark 10:30. Valentinian succeeded Jovian on February 26, 364, and a month later named Valens his colleague. Julian had expelled him from the army officer corps and banished him for failure in duty, or so it was alleged; rumor had it that the real reason was Valentinian's open repugnance for pagan rites (Soz. 6.6.2–6; Theodoret 3.16.1–3; Philostorgius 7.7). Jovian recalled him.

Valens had been baptized by the Homoean Eudoxius of Constantinople (Soc. 4.1.6) and reinstated his creed, which Constantius had officially established toward the end of his reign. He expelled once again all bishops originally banished by Constantius who had returned under Julian's amnesty (Athan. *Hist. Aceph.* 16). The attempt to eject Athanasius, however, met with such popular protest that the order was rescinded after four months and he returned from hiding to remain in tranquil possession of his see until his death (*Hist. Aceph.* 17–18).

Flavius Eutolmius Tatianus was prefect of Egypt 367–370, so *PLRE* 1.876 assumes that the persecution referred to took place in 368–369, and not after Athanasius's death, as Rufinus says. But as Barnes 298 points out, the so-called *Barbarus Scaligeri*, an originally Alexandrian chronicle, lists Tatian as prefect again after Athanasius's death (*Chronica Minora* 1.296).

Apart from these episodes it is hard to substantiate the stories of atrocities planned or committed by Valens which Rufinus and his successors circulated. On Valens's religious policy, cf. H. C. Brennecke, *Studien zur Geschichte der Homöer* (Tübingen, 1988), 181–242. On the stories of his persecutions, cf. ibid., 224–242.

3. Matt 26:50. Athanasius died on May 2, 373. He designated Peter to succeed him a few days before his death (Athan. *Hist. Aceph.* 19). Lucius was a presbyter of George who had led the Arians of Alexandria after George's death; it is not known when and where he was ordained bishop. Peter did not get away immediately after his entry into the city; he was arrested and locked up but later escaped and fled to Rome (Soc. 4.21.4; Soz. 6.19.2, 5).

There is no exaggeration in Rufinus's summary of the scenes which accompanied Lucius's arrival in Alexandria, when the (pagan) governor sent his troops to clear the churches of those loyal to Peter; the grim tale is set out in Peter's own account, quoted copiously by Theodoret (4.22) and supported by Epiphanius (*Pan.* 68.11.4–6). The persecution extended to all the clergy and religious in Egypt who refused to accept Lucius, and it was still going on when Epiphanius was writing the later sections of the *Panarion* (376?).

4. A subtle reference to the "Lives of the Monks" composed originally in Greek (text: A.-J. Festugière, *Historia Monachorum in Aegypto* [Brussels, 1961]) and translated by Rufinus into Latin (text: E. Schulz-Flügel, *Rufinus. Historia Monachorum* [Berlin, 1990]).

On the monks referred to here by name, cf. C. Butler, *The Lausiac History of Palladius* (*Texts and Studies* VI, Cambridge, 1898 and 1904), 2.185, 190–194, 193–194. Macarius the Egyptian (Rufinus *HM* 28), also called "the Elder" or "the Great," is sometimes confused with Macarius of Alexandria (*HM* 29; cf. Thelamon *PC* 380–381). For Isidore, cf. Palladius *HL* 1; for Pambo, *HL* 10.

Oil was often used by the monks for healing; cf. Thelamon *PC* 394. The pagan Egyptians used to come to the temples for healing, and people would scratch some plaster from the walls. The scratches can still be seen, even from times after a temple was Christianized. The water from the temple well, sometimes spoken of as the saliva of the god of the temple, was used for the same purpose; cf. Thelamon PC 384–385. "The lepers in the gospel" refers to Luke 17:17–18.

For the story of Macarius and the hyena, cf. Greek HM 21.15–16; Palladius HL 18.27–28. There are many stories about monks living in peace with wild beasts, especially lions; the underlying theme is the reestablishment of the conditions before the Fall. Cf. Cassian De institutis coenobiorum 9.8; Thelamon PC 389–390.

5. Cf. Soc. 4.24.13–17; Theodoret 4.21.7–14; Soz. 6.20. For other stories of monks converting pagans, cf. Rufinus HM 7.6.5–7.7.9; 9.7.16–20.

6. Cf. Soc. 4.18; Soz. 6.18; Theodoret 4.17.1–4. The official is Domitius Modestus, praetorian prefect of Oriens 369–377. Rufinus's portrait of him as a humane pagan is to be taken with the usual grain of salt. He had been a tepid Christian until Julian's accession, when he converted to paganism, but he returned to Christianity around 365, well before he was appointed praetorian prefect and therefore before this episode; cf. RE 15.2323–2325. Gregory Naz. portrays Rufinus's "vir moderatissimus" as descending upon the churches like a lion to its prey; baptized by the Homoeans, he enthusiastically carried out Valens's measures against the Catholics (Or. 43.48). Cf. note 19.

7. Here Rufinus presents an account not of the conversion of the Saracens to Christianity but of the flourishing of the faith in time of persecution through the merits of a holy person, one of his favorite themes. Mavia's demand for a bishop suggests that she and at least part of her people were already Christian. No reliable ancient source indicates exactly how or when the first Arabs or Saracens were converted; Sozomen records the event as something recent which had taken place through contact with neighboring monks and priests (6.38.14). There were Arabian bishops already at the Councils of Seleucia in 359 (Epiphan. Pan. 73.26.8) and Antioch in 363 (Soc. 3.25.18).

Socrates (4.36.1) and Sozomen (6.38.1) say that Mavia became queen upon her husband's death; the Expositio totius mundi et gentium 20 notes that the Saracens have women rulers. Theophanes' report that Mavia was a Christian captive whom the Saracen king married may be discounted, along with his claim that it was she who requested peace from the Romans (Chron. a.m. 5869).

Mavia's attacks on the Roman frontier are variously explained. Thelamon PC 130 says that they were in retaliation for Julian's refusal to give the Saracens their customary gifts; Ammianus Marcellinus records their attempted raid on the Roman baggage train as a result (25.6.9–10). But this view has been contested by I. Shahîd, Byzantium and the Arabs in the Fourth Century (Washington, 1984), 142–144. Shahîd maintains that Mavia revolted to protest Valens's persecution of the orthodox Christians and to force him to give her people an orthodox bishop. The revolt, in his view, probably took place between 375 and 378. It had to be dealt with quickly, because since 369, when Sapor II had intervened in Armenia, relations with Persia had become strained, and Valens also had to face the Gothic peril. Hence Rufinus's words: "Perurgebat necessitas rei publicae consulendi." As Rufinus says, the peace treaty was successful, cemented not only by Moses' presence but also by the marriage of Mavia's daughter to a Roman general (Soc. 4.36.12); there are other examples of such marriages in the decades following (Thelamon PC 135–136). Mavia later sent Saracen auxiliaries to help defend Constantinople against the Goths after Valens's death (Ammianus Marcellinus 31.16.5; Soc. 5.1; Soz. 7.1.1). Cf. Soc. 4.36; Soz. 6.38; Theodoret 4.23. Cf. also G. W. Bowersock, "Mavia, Queen of the Saracens," *Studien zur Antiken Sozialgeschichte. Festschrift Friedrich Vittinghoff* (Cologne, 1980), 477–495; P. Mayerson, "Mavia, Queen of the Saracens—A Cautionary Note," *Israel Exploration Journal* 30 (1980), 123–131.

8. Luke 18:27.

9. Lev. 11:3.

10. Didymus was born ca. 310–313 and died in 398. He was Rufinus's master and bequeathed to him his admiration for Origen. For his works, cf. P. Nautin, *Encyclopedia of the Early Church*, 235–236. Cf. Palladius *HL* 4; Soz. 3.15.1–5. Antony visited Alexandria for three days in July or August of 338; cf. Athan. *Festal Index* 10; *Life of Antony* 69–71.

11. Rom. 5:20.

12. On the names of the monks and places, cf. Butler, *Lausiac History*, 1.199–203 and 2.187–190. "Alius Paulus in Focis": "Foci" is not identifiable; cf. E. Amélineau, *La géographie de l'Égypte à l'époque copte* (Paris, 1893), 180–181. It is not noticed in A. Calderini, *Dizionario dei nomi geografici e topografici dell' Egitto greco-romano* (Milan, 1987), 5.104.

For Apeliotes, Nitria, Cellulae (or Cellia), and Scete, cf. H. G. Evelyn White, *The Monasteries of the Wâdi 'n Natrûn* (New York, 1932), 2.17–39. Cellulae is described in Rufinus *HM* 22. Nitria is mentioned in *HM* 21, and Pispir and Antony's mountain in Palladius *HL* 21.1.

On the two Macarii, Isidore, and Pambo, cf. 11.4. *HL* has two Moseses at 19 and 39.4. Benjamin is in *HL* 12 and Elias in the Greek *HM* 7.

On the Mesopotamian monks, cf. Theodoret of Cyrrhus, *Histoire des moines de Syrie*, ed. P. Canivet and A. Leroy-Molinghen (Paris, 1977–1979).

13. Zech. 4:11–14.

14. Cf. 2 Cor. 4:7. The errors in Rufinus's biographical sketch of Basil and Gregory are so egregious as to seem almost deliberate, and in fact Thelamon conjectures that he fictionalized the account to make it more edifying (*PC*

441–442). But the words "per annos, ut aiunt, tredecim," do not support this theory; "ut aiunt" suggests Rufinus was drawing on some source, and the specific figure of thirteen years serves no obvious purpose and is found in no known source. C. Moreschini conjectures that he used some life of Gregory now lost ("Rufino traduttore di Gregorio Nazianzeno," *AAAd* 31 [1987], 229).

What is true in Rufinus's account is that both were from noble families and studied together in Athens; Basil was there 349/50–355, and Gregory perhaps 345–356. Basil taught rhetoric in Caesarea (Cappadocia) 355–356, then spent 356 touring the monasteries in Coele Syria, Mesopotamia, Palestine, and Egypt, returned in 357, was baptized in 357/8, and retired to the family estate to lead the ascetic life. He persuaded Gregory, but only after much effort, to join him there in 358; Gregory had been teaching rhetoric in Nazianzus since finishing studies (quite contrary to what Rufinus says). But they were together there for only two years; Gregory's father, the bishop of Nazianzus, brought him back to assist him in his church. Cf. Basil *Ep.* 2 and 14; Gregory Naz. *Ep.* 1, 2, 4, 5, 6; *Carmen de vita sua* 300–311 and 350–356; Gregory Nyssa *Vita S. Macrina* 6; P. J. Fedwick, "A Chronology of the Life and Works of Basil of Caesarea," and J. Gribomont, "Notes biographiques sur s. Basile le Grand," in Fedwick, *Basil of Caesarea: Christian, Humanist, Ascetic* (Toronto, 1981), 3–19 and 21–48; R. Pouchet, *Basile le Grand et son univers d'amis d'après sa correspondance* (Rome, 1992), 6–7; P. Gallay, *La vie de Saint Grégoire de Nazianze* (Paris, 1943).

15. Gregory's father compelled him to accept ordination as presbyter in 361/2. Basil was ordained presbyter probably in 362 by Eusebius of Caesarea, whom he succeeded upon his death in 370. Rufinus's summary of Basil's social and ascetical work is quite accurate; he demanded a high degree of asceticism in those he baptized and constantly urged all Christians to "consecrate their possessions in the churches presided over by the local bishops in order that what is above necessity might be shared with the poor and the needy" (P. Fedwick, *The Church and the Charisma of Leadership in Basil of Caesarea* [Toronto, 1979], 163–164). Cf. also I. Karayannopoulos, "St. Basil's Social Activity," in Fedwick, *Basil of Caesarea: Christian, Humanist, Ascetic*, 375–391.

16. Luke 8:6–7.

17. 2 Cor. 6:10.

18. 1 Cor. 7:32; Phil. 4:5–6; Luke 12:36.

19. Later historians, Rufinus included, conflated the several occasions between 370 and 372 when Valens and various of his officials met or confronted Basil. Cf. R. Van Dam, "Emperor, Bishops, and Friends in Late Antique Cappadocia," *JTS*, n.s., 37 (1986), 53–76.

The prefect in the story is none other than Modestus, encountered earlier in 11.5 doing his best to protect the Catholics from Valens's wrath; cf. note 6.

Gregory of Nyssa relates two attempts he made, mixing threats and promises, to get Basil to accept the emperor's faith (*Contra Eunomium* 1.127–138 and 139–143). In neither case is the order of exile or the emperor's son mentioned. Gregory of Nazianzus likewise reports two such attempts, although the prefect is mentioned explicitly in only the first of them (*Or.* 43.48–51, 54). In the second, Basil is just about to be sent off into exile at night when the emperor's son falls ill; Valens revokes the order of exile and asks Basil to come and pray for him. Basil does so, and the son rallies temporarily but later dies. The incident may have occurred in the spring or summer of 370 or the summer of 371.

For other versions of Basil's reply to the prefect, cf. Gregory Nys. *C. Eunom.* 1.133–135; Gregory Naz. *Or.* 43.48–50. Also Soc. 4.26.16–24; Soz. 6.16; Theodoret 4.19.1–10. On the expulsion of Catholic bishops on Valens's orders and their replacement by Homoeans, cf. Gregory Naz. *Or.* 43.46; Gregory Nys. *C. Eunom.* 1.127–128.

20. Gregory was ordained bishop, much against his will, by Basil and his father in 372. The occasion was Valens's division of the province of Cappadocia into two, leaving Caesarea as the capital of only Cappadocia Prima. The bishop of the *metropolis* or provincial capital, the "metropolitan," had certain powers over the other bishops of the province, and when Tyana was made the capital of the new province of Cappadocia Secunda, its bishop claimed this authority, and independence from Basil. The division of Cappadocia, which probably took place in 371, has often been viewed as a move against Basil, but it may have been done for simple administrative reasons; cf. Van Dam, "Emperor, Bishops, and Friends," 55.

Basil in turn backed his claim to continuing authority over the whole of Cappadocia with the erection of new bishoprics with suffragans loyal to him; he made Gregory bishop of Sasima, a tiny but strategic town. But the bishop of Tyana kept him from taking possession of his see, so he stayed in Nazianzus and assisted his father. At the latter's death in 374, he agreed to take charge of the church in Nazianzus only temporarily, until a successor could be chosen. When this did not happen, he fled to Seleucia in Isauria in 375(?) and stayed there until 379. In this year the Catholics of Constantinople asked him to come to be their bishop, a request he accepted reluctantly. He lodged there in a house he called "Anastasia," which became the church of the Nicene loyalists. He was attacked by other Christian groups, but he drew growing crowds to hear him, among them Jerome.

Theodosius entered Constantinople on November 24, 380; two days later he turned the Homoeans out of the churches, which he handed over to Gregory. The Council of Constantinople, which began in May of 381, elected him bishop of Constantinople, but the bishops of Egypt and Macedonia, when they arrived the following month, protested that the election had been irregular. They probably alleged Canon 15 of Nicaea, which prohibits the transfer of bishops from one see to another. Gregory offered his resignation to the council and to the emperor, and it was accepted (after some hesitation) by Theodosius. His farewell address to the council (*Or.* 42) contains no allusion to Jonah. Rufinus gives a parallel account of Gregory's resignation, with the same allusion, in the preface to his translation of Gregory's discourses (ed. Simonetti, p. 255–256).

Gregory left the city before the end of the council (July 9, 381) and retired to his home in the village of Arianzus. But Nazianzus had still had no bishop since his father had died in 374, and he was pressed to fill the vacancy. He entrusted the church instead to the presbyter Cledonius, but it was troubled by Apollinarian sectarians, and toward the end of 382 Gregory resumed charge of it. The controversies proved too much for him, however, and after requesting his metropolitan in vain for a successor, he simply left Nazianzus for good in 383, retiring once again to Arianzus. His departure forced the issue, and Eulalius was chosen to succeed him. He died ca. 390. Cf. Gallay, *La vie de Saint Grégoire de Nazianze*, 105–243.

21. In the preface to his translation of Basil's sermons, Rufinus gives the number as eight; cf. M. Simonetti, *Tyrannii Rufini Opera* (*CCL* 20, 1961), p. 237. The translation is in *PG* 31.1723–1794. There is some question about just which of Basil's discourses Rufinus meant here; cf. P. J. Fedwick, "The Translations of the Works of Basil before 1400," in his *Basil of Caesarea*, 466–468; H. Marti, "Rufinus' Translation of St. Basil's Sermon on Fasting," *Studia Patristica* 16.2 (1985), 419.

For his translation of Gregory of Nazianzus's discourses, cf. A. Engelbrecht, *Tyrannii Rufini orationum Gregorii Nazianzeni novem interpretatio* (*CSEL* 46, 1910); Moreschini, "Rufino traduttore di Gregorio Nazianzeno," 1.227–285.

For his translation of Basil's monastic rules, cf. K. Zelzer, *Basili Regula* (*CSEL* 86, 1986). The rules seem to have gone through three editions, of which Rufinus translated the second. The Greek original of this has vanished, leaving only the Latin and Syriac translations. A comparison of them shows that Rufinus's is a true translation and not his own invention, as has sometimes been suggested. This second edition, then, known as the *Asceticum Parvum*, was the basis on which Basil himself elaborated his so-called *Asceticum Magnum*. Cf. Zelzer, ix–x; J. Gribomont, *Histoire du texte des Ascétiques de S. Basile* (Louvain, 1953).

"Optantes . . . eorum plura transferre": there is no evidence that he fulfilled his plan; cf. A. di Berardino, *Patrology* 4.252 (Westminster, 1991).

22. Damasus succeeded Liberius on October 1, 366. He had accompanied Liberius into exile in 355, but then returned to Rome and entered into communion with Felix, who had been ordained at court to replace Liberius. After Liberius returned from exile, however, he was reconciled with him. But when Liberius died (September 24, 366), the faction loyal to Felix elected him his successor, while the faction that had remained loyal to Liberius chose the deacon Ursinus. The election was embittered by what was regarded as Liberius's betrayal of Athanasius and of orthodoxy, and by the memory of the Roman clergy's perjury in accepting Felix (cf. Book 10, note 35). Battles took place before and after the election, and Damasus requested help from the city prefect. His partisans attacked the Liberian basilica on October 26, leaving 137 dead. Cf. Ammianus Marcellinus 27.3.12–13; Jerome *Chron.* 366; *Collectio Avellana* 1.5–14; Soc. 4.29; Soz. 6.23.1–2; Kelly *Popes* 32–33.

The bishop who ordained Ursinus was Paul of Tibur (Tivoli); the Basilica of Sicininus is Santa Maria Maggiore.

Flavius Maximinus after various governorships was *praefectus annonae* 368–370, *vicarius urbis* 370–371, and *praefectus praetorio Galliarum* 371–376. He became steadily more brutal and arrogant as his career advanced. His role as judge in sorcery trials made him greatly feared among the nobility during his terms in Rome. Cf. Jones 1.141; *PLRE* 1.577; *RE* suppl. 5 (1933), 663. Rufinus's remark about him remains obscure, however, and as chronologically careless as usual. The emperor banished Ursinus and his partisans (in 368?) to northern Italy, where they continued to disturb the church by slandering Damasus and eventually allying themselves with the Milanese Arians (cf. Ambrose *Ep.* 5(11)). On the whole history of the disputed election and its aftermath, cf. A. Van Roey, "Damase," *DHGE* 14 (1960), 48–50.

23. The Homoean Auxentius had replaced the deposed Dionysius in 355 (cf. 10.21) and had remained in office until his death in 373 or 374, despite the best efforts of Hilary of Poitiers to bring him down. Ambrose was born in Trier in 337 or 339, became a rhetor, and ca. 370 was appointed governor of Liguria and Aemilia, with his residence in Milan. He was consecrated bishop on either December 1, 373, or December 7, 374.

Ambrose mentions his election in *Ep.* 14(63).65, where he says, "Quam resistebam ne ordinarer! Postremo cum cogerer saltem ordinatio protelaretur! Sed not valuit praescriptio, praevaluit impressio. Tamen ordinationem meam occidentales episcopi iudicio, orientales etiam exemplo probarunt. The reference to the Eastern bishops is an allusion to Nectarius of Constantinople, who was elected bishop while still a catechumen (cf. 11.21). It should be noted that Ambrose's biographer Paulinus, normally cited as the standard source for this episode, draws on Rufinus here; cf. M. Pellegrino, *Paolino. Vita di S. Ambrogio*

(Rome, 1961), 16–19. In *De paenitentia* 2.8.67 and *De officiis* 1.1.4 Ambrose talks about how he was "snatched" from life as a civil official to the episcopacy and had to teach before he himself had learned. On his sacramental transition, cf. B. Fischer, "Hat Ambrosius von Mailand in der Woche zwischen seiner Taufe und seiner Bischofskonsekration andere Weihen empfangen?," *Kyriakon, Festschrift Johannes Quasten* (Münster, 1970), 527–531.

Rufinus's is the first formal account of Ambrose's election; was he influenced by Eusebius's report of the election of Fabian (*HE* 6.29.3–4)? Cf. Thelamon *PC* 339. Paulinus adds details such as the child's voice nominating Ambrose and his efforts to dissuade the people (*Vita Ambrosii* 6–9). The emperor, he says, "Summo gaudio adcepit quod iudices a se directi ad sacerdotium peterentur" (8.2).

24. Valentinian died in Illyricum of a stroke on November 17, 375. He had already had his eight-year-old son Gratian proclaimed Augustus in 367 in order to help secure the dynasty. Gratian, now sixteen, succeeded him in Trier. On November 22 government ministers proclaimed Gratian's younger brother Valentinian Augustus in order to secure the loyalty of the Illyrian army. Valentinian, then four, and his mother Justina were staying near Sirmium at the time. Valens and Gratian accepted the move, perhaps after some initial irritation. Cf. Ammianus Marcellinus 30.10; Zosimus 4.19; Ps. Aurelius Victor *Epit.* 45.10; Philostorgius 9.16; Jones 1.140–141.

"Probo tunc praefecto fideliter rem gerente": Petronius Probus was praetorian prefect of Italy, Africa, and Illyricum 368–375 (cf. *PLRE* 1.736–740). Rufinus is the only ancient source to mention him explicitly as the one behind the plan.

25. In 376 the Goths of southern Russia asked to be received into the Roman empire in order to escape the Huns. Valens agreed to accept them and to give them land in Thrace if they would serve in the army. In the autumn of 376 they were ferried across the Danube and a start was made in settling and enrolling them, but as winter came on many of them were still in the transit camp. When provisions ran short, greedy officials began selling them into slavery in return for food. The remaining Ostrogoths, who had not yet gotten permission to cross into Roman territory, took advantage of the ensuing disturbances to cross the river. The last straw was the massacre of a Visigothic escort by a Roman officer; all the Goths rose in revolt and plundered Thrace. Valens met them at Adrianople on August 9, 378, and was routed in a battle which was indeed the "initium mali" for the empire; two-thirds of the Roman army perished there together with the emperor. Cf. Ammianus Marcellinus 31.12–13; Zosimus 4.29.1–2; Jerome *Chron.* 378; *Consularia Constantinopolitana* 378; Soc. 4.38; Soz. 6.39–40.

"annis in imperio cum fratre primo et post cum fratris filiis quattuordecim pariter exactis": another example of Rufinus's chronological carelessness. Valens having come to power in February of 364, he reigned for something less than fourteen years in all. Gratian was named Augustus only in 367, by which time Valentinian II had not yet even been born.

26. "Two are better than one": Eccles. 4:9. Theodosius was born in 347 in Gallaecia. His father distinguished himself as a general under Valentinian I in Britain, Moesia, and Africa, but was executed in Carthage in 375/6 by Valentinian or Gratian for reasons unknown. Theodosius had fought with distinction against the Sarmatians in 374, but he retired to his estate in Spain upon his father's death. Gratian, needing an experienced general as colleague in the wake of the disaster at Adrianople, recalled him and on January 19, 379, proclaimed him Augustus in Sirmium.

"eique orientis procuratione permissa partes sibi ac fratri occiduas reservavit": most of the sources say that the territory given Theodosius corresponds exactly to Valens's old domain, although Sozomen reports that he was given Illyricum as well (7.4.1). Cf. Paschoud 2.386.

Rufinus refers obliquely to Gratian's unpopularity. He had many admirable qualities, but he lacked both interest in administration and advisers who could supply for his inexperience. He alienated the regular army by consorting with his barbarian auxiliaries and adopting their fashions. His fiscal policies, including the withdrawal of financial support for the pagan cults, disaffected the nobility. Magnus Maximus seems to have been *comes Brittaniarum* at the time of his revolt in the spring or summer of 383. When Gratian marched against him his troops abandoned him and he fled with his retinue to Lyons, pursued by Andragathius, *magister equitum* of Maximus, who in the end tricked him into attending a banquet apart from his bodyguard and assassinated him there; the date was August 25. Cf. Zosimus 4.35; Ambrose *In psalm.* 61.24–26; Paschoud 2.412–415.

27. Maximus sent an embassy to Theodosius to offer peace on terms of coexistence and alliance. Theodosius pretended to agree but secretly made preparations to attack him. Cf. Zosimus 4.37; Paschoud 2.422–423.

Justina was the widow of the usurper Magnentius. She married Valentinian ca. 370 and bore him the son who became co-emperor with Gratian at Valens's death. When the Goths overran Thrace after the Battle of Adrianople, she was forced to move with her son from Sirmium to Milan. Once there they requested a church where their Homoean court could worship, and Gratian gave them one. He returned it to the Catholics following the promulgation of *C.Th.* 16.5.6 (January 381), which declared Nicene Catholicism as the only legal religion and outlawed assemblies within cities of Photinians, Arians, and

Eunomians. Cf. D. Williams, "Ambrose, Emperors, and Homoians in Milan: The First Conflict over a Basilica," in *Arianism after Arius*, ed. M. Barnes and D. Williams (Edinburgh, 1993), 127–146.

There is much that remains unclear about where, when, and why the "basilica conflict" took place, and certainly Rufinus is no help. With Gratian dead and Valentinian II only fourteen years old, the empress evidently thought the time was ripe to recover the church she had lost in 381. Around Lent of 385 the consistory ordered Ambrose to yield a basilica, probably the Portiana, so it could be used by the Homoeans. He refused. The demand was then made, as Easter drew near, to give up the New Basilica. Ambrose again refused. Rumors flew, messengers hurried to and from court, troops and police moved about, and the people were gripped by a fever of excitement, but finally on Holy Thursday (April 10) the court gave up.

Sometime later the same year the Homoean bishop Mercurinus Auxentius, who had been deposed from his see of Durostorum by Theodosius, sought refuge with Justina, and together they drafted a law which would permit them to assemble (the project in which Benivolus in 11.16 refused to cooperate). The law, *C.Th.* 16.1.4, of January 23, 386, permits the assemblies of those who hold to the decrees of the Councils of Ariminum (359) and Constantinople (360). On its basis the court on March 27 required Ambrose to hand over the New Basilica. He refused. On the next day the request was made for the Portian Basilica, and the same answer was given. On the following day (Palm Sunday) imperial hangings were put up in the Portian Basilica, but the people flocked to it and remained there until the court gave up its attempt to seize it.

The government apparently made one further try at expropriating a church, probably the Portian Basilica; this is the occasion described by Augustine in *Confessions* 9.7.15 when Ambrose, shut up inside with his flock, taught them the antiphonal singing of psalms to keep up their spirits. Cf. Ambrose *Ep.* 75–77, 75a; F. H. Dudden, *The Life and Times of St. Ambrose* (Oxford, 1935), 270–297; A. D. Lenox-Conyngham, "A Topography of the Basilica Conflict of A.D. 385/6 in Milan," *Historia* 31 (1982), 353–363, and "Juristic and Religious Aspects of the Basilica Conflict of A.D. 386," *Studia Patristica* 18.1 (1985), 55–58; G. Gottlieb, "Der Mailänder Kirchenstreit von 385/6," *Museum Helveticum* 42 (1985), 37–55; G. Nauroy, "Le fouet et le miel. Le combat d'Ambroise en 386 contre l'arianisme milanais," *Recherches augustiniennes* 23 (1988), 3–86; H. Maier, "Private Space as the Social Context of Arianism in Ambrose's Milan," *JTS*, n.s. 45 (1994), 72–93.

28. On Benivolus's part in the drama, cf. note 27, paragraph 4. The *magister memoriae* was a high chancery official responsible for drafting official documents and speeches. Little is otherwise known about Benivolus (cf. *PLRE* 1.161), but

Rufinus's report squares with Gaudentius of Brescia's eulogy of him (*Tractatus Praef.* 5). He retired to private life. The *cingulum* or belt bore the insignia of rank in the civil and military services.

29. Maximus's letter is preserved (*Collectio Avellana* 39); it alludes clearly to Ambrose's recent plight: "Audio . . . novis clementiae tuae edictis ecclesiis catholicis vim illatam fuisse, obsideri in basilicis sacerdotes, multam esse propositam, poenam capitis adiectam et legem sanctissimam sub nomine nescio cuius legis everti" (*CA* 39.3). He made his move toward Italy in the first half of 387, whereupon Valentinian fled by ship to Thessalonica with his mother and sister Galla (cf. Zosimus 4.42—43; Paschoud 2.434).

30. Once arrived in Thessalonica, Justina appealed to Theodosius to restore her son to his realm and promised him the hand of her daughter Galla in exchange. The emperor, recently widowed, was captivated by Galla's beauty and promised to do so on the condition that she and her family renounce the Homoean faith and embrace Catholicism. The deal was struck and Theodosius in the summer of 388 began moving in strength through Upper Pannonia toward Aquileia, where Maximus was staying. Andragathius, his general, had fortified the Alpine passes, but then, persuaded that an attack by sea was imminent, he left the army in order to direct naval operations on the Adriatic. When Theodosius's forces came upon the leaderless army of the usurper, they brushed aside the Alpine defenses and fell upon the main body at Aquileia. The victory was not bloodless (despite what Rufinus pretends in 11.32), but it was quick (Pacatus *Panegyr.* 34.1—2), and Maximus was taken and executed on August 28. Cf. Zosimus 4.44—46; Paschoud 2.436—444; *Panegyr. Lat.* (Mynors) 2(12).32.2—44.2; Orosius *Histor.* 7.35.1—5; Theodoret 5.15.

Justina evidently lived to see her son restored to his throne but died shortly thereafter (Zosimus 4.47.2; Theodoret 7.14.7).

31. The incident took place in the summer of 390 when Butheric, *magister militum per Illyricum*, was lynched by a mob for refusing to release a popular charioteer imprisoned for immorality. Theodosius ordered a massacre of the citizens in reprisal, and then thought better of it and countermanded the order, but it was too late. At least seven thousand were killed in the circus after being treacherously invited there.

News of this reached Ambrose while he was presiding at the Council of Milan of 390, a gathering of Italian and Gallican bishops met to reach a decision about communion with Felix of Trier. The bishops agreed that some reprimand was called for, and Ambrose finally decided to suspend the emperor from communion. His letter to him, a masterpiece of tact, is *Ep.* 11(51). What exactly happened next is not known, but eventually Theodosius did do public penance in church and was readmitted to communion at Christmas.

Cf. Soz. 7.25.1–7; Theodoret 5.17–18.19. The law in question is *C.Th.* 9.40.13; it is dated August 18, 390, so Theodosius had already enacted it before he began his penance.

32. "Theodosius was implacable against heretics: no less than eighteen constitutions directed by him against them are preserved in the Code. In general he went no further than to bar their meetings and confiscate their churches or the private houses in which they held their conventicles" (Jones 1.166).

Sacrifices for divination were forbidden, and the pagans in fact stopped offering sacrifice at all in the temples, which were not, however, officially closed. "But petitions for the demolition of temples or their conversion into churches were favourably received, and a blind eye was turned on unauthorized attacks upon them. The result was that a large number of temples was destroyed, with or without official sanction" (Jones 1.167).

The monk was John of Lycopolis: cf. Greek *HM* 1.1; Rufinus *HM* 1.1; Palladius *HL* 35.2; Thelamon *PC* 342. Eutropius was used as an intermediary; cf. Claudian *In Eutrop.* 1.312–313.

33. Matt. 26:38; Mark 14:34.

34. Apollinaris (ca. 310–ca. 390) became bishop of Laodicea ca. 360 and was a close friend of Athanasius. His doctrine, which sprang from his strong opposition to Arianism, was designed to ensure the immutable sinlessness of Christ. It was condemned by synods in Rome in ca. 374 and 377 and by the Council of Constantinople of 381. Apollinaris seceded from the church ca. 375. Cf. Epiphan. *Pan.* 77; Soc. 2.46.9–11; H. Lietzmann, *Apollinaris von Laodicea und seine Schule* (Tübingen, 1904); E. Mühlenberg, *Apollinaris von Laodicea* (Göttingen, 1969); recent bibliography in R. Hübner, *Die Schrift des Apolinarius von Laodicea gegen Photin (Pseudo-Athanasius, contra Sabellianos) und Basilius von Caesarea* (Berlin, 1989), 289–297.

Lietzmann, *Apollinaris von Laodicea*, 47–48, points out that Rufinus's report on Apollinaris comes from the same well-informed source used by Julian of Eclanum (in Augustine *Opus imperfectum contra Iulianum* 4.47); it may have been Theodore of Mopsuestia's *De incarnatione*.

The Roman synod attended by Damasus and Peter of Alexandria which rejected Apollinaris's teaching (it was not the first to do so, whatever Rufinus says) took place in 377, before Peter's return to Alexandria the following year. Damasus refers to it in his letter to the Eastern bishops in Theodoret 5.10. Rufinus's formulation of its condemnation of the teaching that Christ "lacked anything human or divine" ("vel humanitatis aliquid vel deitatis minus . . . habuisse") corresponds perfectly with the Greek version of Damasus's: ἤτοι ἀνθρωπότητος ἢ θεότητος ἔλαττον ἐσχηκέναι (Theodoret 5.10.5).

Nothing more is known of the Alexandrian synod which confirmed the Roman sentence. The synodal document of the Council of Constantinople (381) which condemned Apollinaris has not survived; cf. Lietzmann, *Apolinaris von Laodicea*, 30.

35. The terms of office of the bishops mentioned are: Siricius, 384–399; Peter II of Alexandria, 373–381; Timothy I, 381–385; Theophilus, 385–412; John of Jerusalem, 386–417; Flavian I of Antioch, 381–404; Nectarius of Constantinople, 381–397.

On the schism in Antioch, cf. Book 10, note 37. "ipsisque in hoc elementis terrae marisque fatigatis" refer to the innumerable journeys by land and sea undertaken by various parties in the effort to achieve reconciliation.

Nothing further is known of this Diodore of Tyre; he is mentioned in Athan. *Ep.* 64 (*PG* 26.1261).

The courtly Nectarius succeeded Gregory of Nazianzus (cf. 11.9 and note 20). Sozomen 7.8, in what is by far the fullest account of his election, makes him the emperor's choice, Socrates 5.8.12 the people's. The two accounts are not of course irreconcilable.

36. Cf. Deut. 32:33; 1 Cor. 10:21.

37. "ad templum quasi ad arcem quandam refugiebant": Soz. 7.15.3 says that it was the Serapeum.

38. The destruction by the Christians of Alexandria of the great temple of Serapis in 391 had been foreshadowed by the antipagan campaign pursued so ardently by the praetorian prefect Cynegius in Egypt and elsewhere during his term of 384–388 (cf. Paschoud 2.424–426). Christian monks throughout his territory had pillaged and destroyed rural and even urban shrines, although no law existed justifying such acts (Libanius *Or.* 30.8–23). Even so, the razing of the most splendid temple of antiquity sent a shock through the empire; the story of the violent end of Serapis and his house, which Rufinus begins here, was repeated endlessly and lost nothing in the telling, symbolizing as it did the replacement of paganism by Christianity as the official religion of the state. It tended in fact to gather and assimilate to itself other stories of other Christian attacks on Egyptian paganism from the time of George of Alexandria onward, a tendency to which Rufinus's habitual carelessness with chronology gladly lent itself. For a study of the ancient sources and their relationships, cf. Baldini.

Rufinus gives it more attention than any other event for this reason, and also perhaps because of the close relationship between Egypt and Aquileia, the city through which the Egyptian cults were introduced to the north of Italy and beyond (cf. M.-C. Budischovsky, "La diffusion des cultes égyptiens d'Aquilée à travers les pays alpins," *AAAd* 9 [1976], 202–227, and "Les cultes orientaux à Aquilée et leur diffusion en Istrie et en Vénétie," *AAAd* 12 [1977], 99–123; F. Cassola, "Aquileia e l'Oriente mediterraneo," *AAAd* 12 [1977], 67–97; C. Dolzani, "Presenze di origine egiziana nell'ambiente aquileiese e nell'alto adriatico," *AAAd* 12 [1977], 125–134).

Even in his account the distinction is still just visible between the events taking place in the episcopates of George (alluded to in the reference to Constantius's "bishops") and of Theophilus (referred to finally at the end of 11.26). George's hostility to pagan temples and his desire to acquire their property is well attested. Julian says that the Alexandrians were provoked to lynch George when he seized the Serapeum with the prefect's help and stripped it of its statues and decorations (*Ep.* 60.379AB). It is evident that he did not destroy the temple, or Julian would have mentioned that as an even better excuse for leniency toward the Alexandrians, and that Julian restored to the shrine of his great patron the objects George had removed. In Ammianus Marcellinus 22.11.7–8, George is heard to wonder aloud how long the temple of the Genius will stand, a remark which stuns the bystanders and forms in them the resolve to do away with him at the first chance. Whether or not the "temple of the Genius" was the Serapeum is disputed (Baldini 130 note 70). Socrates 3.2 (paralleled by Soz. 5.7.5–6) says that Constantius donated a ruined Mithreum to George, who discovered some grisly cultic relics in its cellars while it was being purified. He paraded them through the streets and thereby incited the pagans to riots and the murder of Christians, who then gave up converting the Mithreum to their own use. But the pagans harbored their anger and at the first opportunity (when Constantius's death was announced) proceeded to lynch George. The various accounts are not irreconcilable. George was rumored to have cast greedy eyes on all the temples of Alexandria (Ammianus 22.11.6), and he might well have provoked its citizens by all of the acts reported of him.

As for Theophilus, the relationship between his actions and the policies of Theodosius is not altogether clear. Cynegius's activities in Egypt (cf. *Consularia Constantinopolitana* 388) would have encouraged the idea that the emperor turned a blind eye toward attacks on idols, but none of Theodosius I's surviving laws authorize them, not even *C.Th.* 16.10.11 of June 16, 391. This edict applied to Egypt the ban on pagan worship contained in *C.Th.* 16.10.10 of February 24, 391, and was issued in response to the riots described by Rufinus here. It was forbidden to visit temples, worship idols, offer incense or libations to them, and perform animal sacrifices; but the destruction of temples is prescribed neither here nor in any other edict. Thus the parallel account in Soc. 5.16, which begins by saying that the emperor ordered the demolition, under Theophilus's supervision, of the temples in Alexandria, must be treated with caution. No reason is given for the order, and no disturbances occur when the Serapeum is brought down; only when the cultic objects are displayed in public do the riots begin. The account thus sounds confused, despite (or perhaps because of) being based on eyewitness reports (5.16.9, 13–14). Sozomen, however, does agree that the emperor ordered the demolition of the Alexandrian temples (7.15.7); Rufinus is vaguer, but his words in context suggest the same. The question, therefore, of whether Theodosius did in fact issue such an order must remain undecided, as must that of the reason for his sudden turn against paganism evident in the edicts of 391. On this cf. *RE* Suppl. 13.891–892, 956–958; *RAC* 13.1160–1161.

Sozomen, in contrast to the other two historians, says that it was a temple of Dionysus which Theophilus was purifying and which yielded from its cellars the cultic items the display of which caused the riot. But from then on his account parallels Rufinus's closely. J. Schwartz, "La fin du Sérapéum d'Alexandrie," *Essays in Honor of C. Bradford Welles* (New Haven, 1966), 109, suspects that their reports of the strife preceding the destruction of the statue of Serapis are just reproductions of events which took place in George's time.

On the philosopher Olympus or Olympius, cf. *Damascii Vitae Isidori Reliquiae*, ed. C. Zintzen (Hildesheim, 1967), fr. 91, 93–94, 97.

The government officials involved in the episode remain anonymous in Rufinus's account, but we learn from Eunapius *Vit. Philosoph.* 472 and Soz. 7.15.5 that Evagrius was prefect of Egypt at the time; Romanus was *comes Aegypti*. It was they to whom *C.Th.* 16.10.11 was addressed.

Sophronius's account of the destruction of the Serapeum (cf. Jerome *De viris illustribus* 134) may have been one of Rufinus's sources.

39. Another ancient description of the Serapeum is offered by Aphthonius of Antioch; cf. *Aphthonii Progymnasmata*, ed. H. Rabe [Leipzig, 1926], pp. 38–41 with the commentary of John of Sardis, ed. H. Rabe [Leipzig, 1928], p. 227–230. Cf. also Ammianus Marcellinus 22.16.12–13; *Expositio totius mundi et gentium* 35f. For a description of the statue and its origin, cf. Clement Alex. *Protrept.* 4.48.

Archaeology throws some light on Rufinus's description; cf. Rowe and Rees, esp. 486–488. The temple in his account was a structure of Roman date built over the remains of another smaller one of the Ptolemaic period. Thus the words "cuncta . . . quoad summum pavimentorum evadatur" refer to the lower and upper levels resulting from the Roman renovation, which included the high column standing on the upper plateau. The rooms below it were illuminated by ceiling lights. "The rooms may have been two-storeyed, the roof of the upper storey being on a level with the uppermost parts of the enclosure on the plateau above" (Rowe and Rees, 488).

ἀγνεύοντες is an imprecise term, since it could refer to those dedicated either temporarily or permanently to various forms of abstinence; cf. Thelamon *PC* 203–205. The temple ministers are described in *Expositio mundi* 36.

We cannot be sure of the provenance of the great statue of Serapis; cf. Thelamon *PC* 173–175.

40. The existence of the window is confirmed by Alexandrian coinage, and the same arrangement for sun and window is found in other Egyptian temples. The Egyptians thought of the sun as reviving the statues of gods by shining on them and thus recharging them with vital force. The image of the sun kissing Serapis is found on coins and lamps of the period; cf. Thelamon *PC* 183–184, 195–197.

The use of magnets in temple ceilings for the purpose Rufinus describes is well attested; cf. Claudian *Magnes* 22–39; Pliny *Natural History* 34.42 (a magnet in the ceiling of an Alexandrian temple); Ausonius *Mosella* 315–317; Augustine *City of God* 21.6.; Thelamon *PC* 182, 184.

41. The Egyptians feared the world would collapse in chaos if the customary rites were not performed; cf. Thelamon *PC* 200, note 19 (papyrological evidence); *Corpus Hermeticum*, Asclepius 24; Ps. Jamblicus *De mysteriis* 6.7; Epiphan. *Pan.* 18.3.1–2.

The description of the soldier with the axe sounds like Valerius Maximus's story of the destruction of the temple of Serapis in Rome (1.3.4): "L. Aemilius Paulus consul, cum senatus Isidis et Serapis fana diruenda censuisset, eaque nemo opificum adtingere auderet, posita praetexta securem arripuit templique eius foribus inflixit." Eunapius *Vit. Philosoph.* 472 attests that the Serapeum was razed to the ground on this occasion. For another version of the story, cf. Theodoret 5.22.3–6.

For the bushel (*modius*) with which Serapis was crowned, cf. note 42.

42. Serapis was originally Ousor-Hapi, the Memphite god of the dead, represented as a mummified man with a bull's head bearing the solar disk surmounted by two feathers between the horns. The Greeks at first called him Osorapis. He was assimilated to Jupiter and to the sun; cf. Thelamon *PC* 189, 193. For the pagan traditions about him, cf. Tacitus *Hist.* 4.84; Plutarch *De Iside* 61.376A; Clement Alex. *Protrept.* 4.48.6.

Rufinus connects the words *modius* ("bushel"), *modus* ("restraint"), and *moderari* ("govern"): "cum mensura modoque cuncta . . . moderari." The bushel-crown is a reminder of the connection of Serapis with Osiris, the god of grain. It was also a symbolic Nile measure, since the crops depended on the seasonal flooding of the river; cf. Thelamon *PC* 191–192.

One tradition connecting Joseph with Serapis derives from his ancestry: he is Σάρρας παῖς (Firmicius Maternus *De errore profanarum religionum* 13.2). Cf.

also Tertullian *Ad nationes* 2.8.9–18; Paulinus of Nola *Carmen* 19.100–106. Firmicius Maternus *De errore profanarum religionum* 13.2 says that the Egyptians divinized Joseph, transforming him into Serapis, and crowned him with the bushel to commemorate his feeding of the people.

Apis was connected with Memphis in Greek legend, as Rufinus says; Clement of Alexandria, for instance, says that Apis, king of Argos, founded Memphis, also called Serapis (*Strom.* 1.106.4–5). Epiphan. *Pan.* 4.2.6 equates Apis with Inachus, who built Memphis. Rufinus, however, is the only one who ascribes a donation of food to him; perhaps he is assuming a connection with Joseph.

The Hapi-bull was originally a fertility god, as Rufinus suggests. When he was slain after his allotted lifetime, a diligent search was conducted for his successor, which could be identified by the marks on its hide, especially the image of a crescent moon; the priestly scribes knew how to verify them. After being weaned, the calf was taken to Memphis, raised amid every luxury in a sacred enclosure, and treated as divine. Cf. Ammianus Marcellinus 22.14.6–8; Aelian *De natura animalium* 11.10.

The derivation of "Serapis" from σορός and "Apis" is found also in Plutarch *De Iside* 29.362C (along with other derivations) and in Clement Alex. *Strom.* 1.106.6.

43. Human sacrifice, especially of virgins and children for the purpose of extispicy, is well enough attested for classical antiquity and afterward, although some of the literary references are hard to evaluate. Didius Julianus, when he was emperor in 193, is reported frequently to have killed children as part of a magic rite to find out the future (Dio Cassius 74.16.5). Sextus Empiricus mentions human sacrifice still being practiced ca. 200 (3.24.221). Ammianus Marcellinus reports an officer being convicted (in 371/2) of eviscerating a woman in order to perform haruspicy on her fetus (29.2.17). Eusebius cites Dionysius of Alexandria on the extispicy performed on children by Valerian (*HE* 7.10.14). Other references are fictional, such as *Historia Augusta* Heliogabalus 8.1–2 and the horrifying scene in Achilles Tatius *Leucippe* 3.15, 19. The emperor Julian and his followers were often accused by the Christians of such things; cf. Theodoret 3.26; Soc. 3.13.11; John Chrysostom *De S. Babyla* 79. For Egypt, cf. J. G. Griffiths, "Human Sacrifices in Egypt: The Classical Evidence," *Annales du service des antiquités de l'Égypte* 48 (1948), 409–423. Archaeology has discovered the use of urns to bury the remains of child sacrifices in North Africa; cf. J. B. Rives, "Tertullian on Child Sacrifice," *Museum Helveticum* 51 (1994), 54–63, esp. 60.

44. The story sounds like that of Paulina and Decius Mundus told by Josephus (*Antiquities* 18.65–80). Saturn/Kronos is identified by Plutarch with

Anubis (*De Iside* 44.368E), the god whom Decius Mundus pretended to be. Josephus in turn is influenced by Ps. Callisthenes *Historia Alexandri Magni* 1.4–6. Many examples have been found of statues hollowed out from behind so that priests could speak through them; cf. Thelamon *PC* 241–242.

45. Contests between magicians were not uncommon in this age. In Chaldaean theurgy, fire was the primal and sacred principle; the Egyptians, by contrast, revered water as the source of life. The Nile was assimilated to Osiris, whose enemy was Set, later identified with Typhon. He was the principle of dryness and thus of death, a fiery, serpentine deity whose color, red, was also that of the desert he inhabited.

Canopus was the name of both the city and the god, who was represented as a potbellied jar with the head of Osiris; since Osiris was worshiped at Canopus in this form, the very name "Canopus" came to be applied to this deity; cf. Thelamon *PC* 207–208. Canopus had been Menelaus's helmsman; he died in Egypt of snakebite during the voyage home from the Trojan War and was buried where the city later sprang up. Cf. Strabo 17.1.17; Ammianus Marcellinus 22.16.14; Hecataeus of Miletus *Fragmente der Griechischen Historiker* (Jacoby) I, fr. 308. What Rufinus offers, then, is some version of an originally etiological myth of the Canopus shrine: the victory of Osiris over the power of fire and of Canopus over the serpentine god that had killed him. Cf. Thelamon *PC* 211–213, 224.

The city was famous as a pleasure resort; cf. Strabo and Ammianus Marcellinus 22.16.14. The original Egyptian name Kahi-Noub was still remembered; cf. Aelius Aristid. *Or.* 36.109. It also had several temples of great renown which as usual were also schools for the teaching of sacred writing; the characters composing it were regarded as holding magic powers. To learn hieroglyphics was to learn the magic formulas contained in them (Thelamon *PC* 226).

Perspiring statues were widely known in antiquity. The waters of the Nile were regarded as the bodily fluids of Osiris, which were believed to be preserved in a jar kept in the Eighteenth Nome. Examples from Egypt of representing gods as jars with heads goes back to the Pharaonic age (Thelamon *PC* 210, 220).

46. It was usual for Christians to call pagan temples "cemeteries" or "burial grounds." Eunapius *Vit. Philosoph.* 472 records the settlement of monks in Canopus after the destruction of the temple there and the building of a martyr's shrine. The church to which Rufinus refers was known as the Angelium or Evangelium (Thelamon *PC* 264).

47. Julian himself mentions pagan attacks on Christians: *Misopogon* 357C, 361A; *Ep.* 114.438B. Cf. also Soz. 7.21.1; Philostorgius 7.4; *Chronicon Pasch.* 295CD.

On the belief that the relics of John the Baptist were located in Sebaste, cf. Jerome *Ep.* 46.13, 108.13. According to another tradition recorded in Soz. 7.21, the head of John the Baptist was found by monks of Jerusalem and was eventually brought to Constantinople in Theodosius's time. This report does not necessarily contradict that of Rufinus', who seems to represent an Alexandrian tradition authenticating and advertising the Baptist's relics and shrine built by Theophilus. In fact, Rufinus may have drawn from Theophilus's own writing on the subject; cf. T. Orlandi, *Storia della chiesa di Alessandria* (Milan, 1967), 1.94–96, 1.120–121; Baldini 124 note 57, 136 note 83, 144.

The title "supreme pontiff" (*pontifex maximus* or *summus*) was commonly applied to bishops; cf., for example, *EOMIA* 1.254.

"Parentinae urbis": Mommsen reads this rather than "Palestinae urbis." Other bishops of Parentium (in Istria) are unknown between Maurus, who was martyred (in Diocletian's time?), and the sixth-century Euphrasius; cf. Thelamon *PC* 292–293.

48. The site of the Alexandrian Serapeum was used to build a church named after Theodosius's son Arcadius (Soz. 7.15.10). On the conversion of the temple of Isis in Menuthis, near Canopus, into a church of the Evangelists, cf. P. Athanassiadi, "Persecution and Response in Late Paganism," *Journal of Hellenic Studies* 113 (1993), 15. See also Rufinus *HM* 7.7 (conversion by the monk Apollonius of pagans, who burn their idol).

49. Putting the sign of the cross on pagan temples to exorcise their gods, which the Christians believed to be demons, was normal procedure, as archeology reveals. The *ankh* symbol, to which Rufinus refers, and which with several variations was cruciform, meant "life" in Egyptian; the gods and goddesses are represented holding it, or holding it to the nostrils of dead kings. The ancient Greek texts translate it as "eternal life." The Egyptian Christians were aware of this meaning and consciously adopted it as a sign of the cross which divine Providence had arranged to appear among the hieroglyphics. Cf. Thelamon *PC* 271–272.

According to another account in Soc. 5.17 and Soz. 7.15.10, the cruciform sign was found in the ruins of the Serapeum and occasioned numerous conversions among the pagans.

On prophecies of the destruction of pagan religion and of the temples of Isis and Serapis, cf. Clement Alex. *Protrept.* 4.50 (*Or. Sib.* 5.484–485, 487–488); *Corpus Hermeticum* Asclepius 24; Eunapius *Vit. Philosoph.* 473.

50. During the civilizing of the Nile valley, Nilometers seem to have been installed within the precincts of various temples scattered along the length of the river in Egypt, thus allowing accurate measurement of the annual flood from the time and place the waters began to rise. Such measurement was es-

sential to irrigation control and harvest forecasts (and thus to tax levies). The Nilometers used for this purpose, unlike the ceremonial instrument to which Rufinus refers, were water scales chiseled on walls where the river would reach or on columns erected in cisterns; the cisterns were connected with the river by pipes and furnished with windows and lamps for illumination. Archeology has discovered on some Nilometers a small rectangular recess to mark the height the water had to reach for proper irrigation; the announcement that it had been reached was the signal for one of the great religious feasts of the year.

The role played in all of this by the πῆχυς or *ulna* mentioned by Rufinus is not altogether clear. A portable cubit-rule seems of little use in measuring the rise of a river. But archeology has found indications that the wooden "sacred cubit" was in fact kept within the Nilometer, and perhaps within the recess mentioned above. It was carried in the annual procession celebrating the river rise, together with a golden vase holding the new water, and that is what Rufinus must mean when he talks about bringing the gauge to the temple. The procession began and ended in the Serapeum; otherwise its route is unknown. Thelamon thinks that when Rufinus mentions the temple where the procession ended ("mensura . . . ad templum Serapis [deferebatur]"), he means the temples of Serapis in each place along the Nile (over a dozen in all), each of which helped measure the flood (*PC* 276–277). The Alexandrian Serapeum itself was hardly suited to accurate river measurement because of its location, although it did have a Nilometer in an underground cistern connected with the subterranean aqueducts of the ancient city; the aqueducts were fed from the "Canal of Alexandria." But it may have been the administrative center of flood control for the whole country.

On the measurement of the Nile and irrigation, cf. Pliny *Natural History* 5.10.57–58. On Nilometers, cf. H. Jaritz, "Wasserstandsmessungen am Nil—Nilometer," *Mitteilungen aus dem Leichtweiss-Institut für Wasserbau* 89 (Braunschweig, 1986, no consecutive pagination). On the Alexandrian Nilometer, cf. F. E. Engreen, "The Nilometer in the Serapeum at Alexandria," *Medievalia et humanistica* 1 (1943), 3–13; Rowe and Rees 492. On the Nile festival and procession, cf. D. Bonneau, *La crue du Nil* (Paris, 1964), 429–430.

Much remains unclear about the process of transferring this vast system of water control from temple to church. Constantine is reported to have abolished the Nile priesthood and moved the cubit-rule to the church, with no diminishment of the annual flood, predictions to the contrary notwithstanding (Eusebius *VC* 4.25; Soc. 1.18.2–3). Julian later restored the measuring rod to the Serapeum (Soz. 5.3.3), where the traditional rites to ensure the flood were still going on when Libanius wrote *Pro templis* in 386 (cf. *Or.* 30.35). Guardianship of the ceremonial "Nilometer" was obviously important, but did it bring with it effective control of the whole irrigation system, with the considerable political and economic power that would have meant? Athanasius, for instance, was at least reputed to wield great economic influence (*Apol. contra Arianos* 9.3–4; 18.2, 60.2, 87.1); is this part of the reason? The difficulty is that control of the irrigation system implies supervision of the network of Nilometer temples, and it is hard to imagine the bishop of Alexandria, even such a one as Athanasius, achieving this without the conversion of the temple staffs to Christianity, a conversion which evidently took place only in Theophilus's time.

The close connection between the Nile flood-control system and the temples was partly religious. The Nile was held to be divine; the rites in his honor were meant to ensure that he fertilized the land each year (Libanius *Pro templis*; Tertullian *Ad nationes* 1.9.3 and *Apologeticum* 40.2; Aelius Aristid. *Or.* 45.32). But it was also partly technical; the temple staffs were those trained to use and maintain the Nilometer system, and it may be supposed that they took care to preserve their indispensability. Hence Rufinus's passing mention in 11.29 of the conversion of these staffs ("hi, qui erant ex sacerdotibus vel ministris templorum") suggests that at least in Theophilus's time, effective control of the Nile did pass to the church, with all that that meant. The pagan Nile feasts were replaced by Christian ones; in each place the cult of the river god was replaced by that of the local saint or St. Michael (Thelamon *PC* 277). Bonneau, *La crue du Nil*, 435–439 describes the Christianization of the liturgy of the Nile rise. A monograph on the subject of the Nile River and the bishop of Alexandria would be most useful.

The harm which Theodosius exclaims the city has escaped has been variously interpreted to mean the high flood waters Rufinus mentions or the religious riot described earlier.

51. Arbogast was a barbarian, perhaps of Frankish stock, who had risen to the position of *comes rei militaris* or perhaps *vicarius magistri militum* when Gratian sent him in 380 to help Theodosius against the Goths. Theodosius kept him and included him in his staff, perhaps with the rank of *magister militum*, in the campaign against Maximus in 388. Following the usurper's defeat, he was sent to Gaul to deal with his son and stayed in the West as Valentinian's guardian and regent.

The present episode took place in the spring of 392 in Vienne, by which time Arbogast certainly held the rank of *magister militum*; a couple of sources say he assumed the title without permission. Valentinian died on May 15, 392, after a period of fruitlessly trying to assert himself in the government of his territory; he was twenty years old. The sources are divided on whether it was murder or suicide, and the question can no longer be decided. Cf. Zosimus 4.53–54; Soc. 5.25.1–5; Soz. 7.22.2; Philostorgius 11.1; John of Antioch, *Excerpta de insidiis* fr. 79; B. Croke, "Arbogast and the Death of Valentinian II," *Historia* 25 (1976), 235–244; Paschoud, 2.452–458; G. Zecchini, "Barbari e romani in Rufino di Concordia," *AAAd* 31 (1987), 2.43–44.

The embassy was sent in the autumn of 392 in an attempt to avoid civil war; cf. Zosimus 4.55.3–4; *Excerpta de insidiis* fr. 79; Paschoud 2.459.

52. On the monk John, cf. 11.19. On Theodosius's victory over Maximus, cf. 11.17 and note 30.

53. Arbogast was a sincere pagan, and with the death of Valentinian II and the break with Theodosius, a pagan revival made itself felt in the West in 393–394. Eugenius, the nominal usurper, had no military connections and no influence, and for that very reason he was picked by Arbogast, who as a barbarian could not hope to succeed to the throne. Eugenius had been a teacher of grammar or rhetoric and then a chancery bureau chief; he was not pagan, whatever some sources may suggest. Virius Nicomachus Flavianus, by contrast, was one of the leaders of the pagan revival; praetorian prefect of Italy, Africa, and Illyricum, he had published a prediction that Christianity was to last only a year of years and thus to end in 394 (Augustine *City of God* 18.53; cf. also Soz. 7.22.4–5).

When Rufinus refers to the flight of the demons, he means the statues of Jupiter erected in the Alpine passes and the image of Hercules at the head of Eugenius's army. The two gods were patrons of the pagan revival, as they had been of the Tetrarchy; Hercules' temple in Ostia had been restored in the summer of 394. Cf. Thelamon *PC* 317. On Arbogast's trust in idols, cf. Paulinus *Vita Ambrosii* 31.1–3.

The battle lasted two days, ending with Eugenius's death on September 6, 394. It took place at Fluvium Frigidum, thirty-six miles from Aquileia on the route to Emona. The ancient accounts of the battle, in addition to Zosimus 4.58, are collected in Paschoud 2.488–500. Commentary: Paschoud 2.467–468, 474–487. Rufinus's source may have been Paulinus of Nola's lost panegyric on Theodosius's victory; cf. Zecchini, "Barbari e romani," 2.46–49.

54. Cf. Ps. 115:2. Other sources say that Theodosius's enemies drew up their lines in the plain. Rufinus's words "in descensu montis" suggest that they were right at the foot of the mountain. On the ambush and the location of the gorge in question, cf. Paschoud 2.482–483. Eugenius's troops, hidden in ambush by the top of the pass, allowed Theodosius's forces to march by and then moved in to occupy the position, thus trapping the emperor between themselves and the usurper. Theodosius, meanwhile, engaged the enemy in front of him with his Gothic allies, 10,000 of whom were lost when they were trapped in a gorge;

he thus had plenty to pray about when night fell. But during the night or in the morning, the enemy occupying the top of the pass defected to him. His staff advised him to fall back on Illyricum and regroup, but he believed the defection was an answer to his prayers and decided to push forward; cf. Paschoud 2.483–484.

55. On Bacurius, cf. 10.11 and note 22. On the miraculous wind, cf. Ambrose *In Ps.* 36.25.

56. Cf. Zosimus 4.59. Honorius had already been given the rank of Augustus on January 23, 393, in Constantinople; cf. Paschoud 2.468. Theodosius died on January 17, 395, in Milan, having been made Augustus in January of 379.

# ABBREVIATIONS

| | |
|---|---|
| AAAd: | *Antichità altoadriatiche* |
| *ANRW:* | *Aufstieg und Niedergang der römischen Welt* |
| Athan. *De decretis,* etc.: | Athanasius, *De decretis Nicaenae synodi, Apologia contra Arianos, Historia Arianorum, De synodis* |
| Baldini: | A. Baldini, "Problemi della tradizione sulla 'distruzione' del Serapeo di Alessandria," *Rivista storica dell'antichità* 15 (1985), 97–152. |
| Barnes: | T. D. Barnes, *Athanasius and Constantius* (Cambridge, MA, 1993). |
| CCL: | Corpus Christianorum, Series Latina |
| CSEL: | Corpus Scriptorum Ecclesiasticorum Latinorum |
| *C.Th.:* | *Theodosian Code* |
| Cassian *Coll.:* | John Cassian, *Collationes* |
| *DEC:* | *Decrees of the Ecumenical Councils* (ed. N.P. Tanner, London, 1990) |
| *DHGE:* | *Dictionnaire d'histoire et de géographie ecclésiastiques* |
| *EOMIA:* | *Ecclesiae Occidentalis Monumenta Iuris Antiquissima,* ed. C. H. Turner (Oxford, 1899–1939). |
| Epiphan. *Pan.:* | Epiphanius, *Panarion* |
| Eusebius, *HE:* | Eusebius, *Church History* |
| Eusebius *VC:* | *Vita Constantini* |

Hanson: R. P. C. Hanson, *The Search for the Christian Doctrine of God* (Edinburgh, 1988).

Hefele-Leclercq: C. J. Hefele and H. Leclercq, *Histoire des conciles d'après les documents originaux* (Paris, 1907–1952).

Hilary *Frag.*: Hilary, *Collectanea antiariana parisina*, ed. A. Feder, *Corpus Scriptorum Ecclesiasticorum Latinorum* 65 (1916).

*HM*: *Historia Monachorum* (Greek text; "Rufinus *HM*" refers to Rufinus's translation)

Jones: A. H. M. Jones, *The Later Roman Empire* (Oxford, 1964)

*JRS*: *Journal of Roman Studies*

*JTS*: *Journal of Theological Studies*

Kelly *Popes*: J. N. D. Kelly, *Oxford Dictionary of the Popes* (Oxford, 1986).

Klein: R. Klein, *Constantius II und die christliche Kirche* (Darmstadt, 1977).

Opitz *Urk.*: *Athanasius Werke* 3.1. *Urkunden zur Geschichte des Arianischen Streites 318–328*, ed. H.-G. Opitz (Berlin, 1934).

Palladius *HL*: *Historia Lausiaca*

Paschoud: F. Paschoud, *Zosime. Histoire nouvelle* (Paris, 1971–1989).

*PG*: *Patrologia Graeca*

Philostorgius: Philostorgius, *Church History*

*PL*: *Patrologia Latina*

*PLRE*: *Prosopography of the Later Roman Empire*, ed. Jones, Martindale, and Morris (Cambridge, 1971ff.).

*RAC*: *Reallexikon für Antike und Christentum*

*RE*: *Real-Encyclopädie der classischen Altertumswissenschaft*

Rowe and Rees: A. Rowe and B. R. Rees, "A Contribution to the Archaeology of the Western Desert: IV," *Bulletin of the John Rylands Library* 39.2 (1957), 485–520.

Rufinus, *HM*: Rufinus, *Historia Monachorum*

Schwartz: E. Schwartz, *Gesammelte Schriften* (Berlin, 1938–1963).

Soc.: Socrates, *Church History*

Soz.: Sozomen, *Church History*

Stein-Palanque: Stein-Palanque, *Histoire du Bas-Empire* (Bruges, 1959).

Thelamon *PC*: F. Thelamon, *Païens et chrétiens au IV$^e$ siècle* (Paris, 1981).

Theodoret: Theodoret, *Church History*

Zecchini: G. Zecchini, "Barbari e romani in Rufino di Concordia," *AAAd* 31 (1987), 2.29–60.

*ZNW*: *Zeitschrift für die neutestamentliche Wissenschaft und die Kunde des Urchristentums*

# BIBLIOGRAPHY

GENERAL

Alonso-Nuñez, José Miguel, "Die Auslegung der Geschichte bei Paulus Orosius: Die Abfolge der Weltreiche, die Idee der Roma Aeterna und die Goten," *Wiener Studien* 106 (1993), 197–213.

Amélineau, E., *La géographie de l'Égypte à l'époque copte* (Paris, 1893).

Athanassiadi, Polymnia, "Persecution and Response in Late Paganism," *Journal of Hellenic Studies* 113 (1993), 1–29.

Aubert, R., "Hilaire," *DHGE* 24.459–461.

Avi-Jonah, Michael, *The Jews of Palestine* (Oxford, 1976).

Baldini, Antonio, "Problemi della tradizione sulla 'distruzione' del Serapeo di Alessandria," *Rivista storica dell'antichità* 15 (1985), 97–152.

Bardy, G., "Cyrille de Jérusalem," *DHGE* 13.1181–1186.

Barnes, Michael R. and Daniel H. Williams (ed.), *Arianism after Arius* (Edinburgh, 1993)

Barnes, Timothy D., *Athanasius and Constantius* (Cambridge, MA, 1993).

Bartelink, G. J. M., ed., *Vie d'Antoine. Athanase* (Paris, 1994).

———, *Vita di Antonio* (Milan, 1974).

Bell, H. Idris, *Jews and Christians in Egypt* (London, 1924).

Bihain, Ernest, "La source d'un texte de Socrate (HE 2.38.2) relatif à Cyrille de Jérusalem," *Byzantion* 32 (1962), 81–91.

Bonneau, Danielle, *La crue du Nil* (Paris, 1964).

Bowersock, Glen W., "Limes Arabicus," *Harvard Studies in Classical Philology* 80 (1976), 219–229.

———, "Mavia, Queen of the Saracens," *Studien zur antiken Sozialgeschichte. Festschrift Friedrich Vittinghoff* (Cologne, 1980), 477–495.

Breen, Aidan, "A New Irish Fragment of the *Continuatio* to Rufinus-Eusebius *Historia Ecclesiastica*," *Scriptorium* 41 (1987), 185–204.

Brennecke, H. C., *Hilarius von Poitiers und die Bischofsopposition gegen Konstantius II* (Berlin, 1984).

———, *Studien zur Geschichte der Homöer* (Tübingen, 1988).

Brock, S. P., "Rebuilding of the Temple under Julian: A New Source," *Palestine Exploration Quarterly* (1976), 103–107.

Budischovsky, M.-C., "La diffusion des cultes égyptiens d'Aquilée à travers les pays alpins," *AAAd* 9 (1976), 202–227.

———, "Les cultes orientaux à Aquilée et leur diffusion en Istrie et en Vénétie, *AAAd* 12 (1977), 99–123.

Butler, Dom Cuthbert, *The Lausiac History of Palladius* (*Texts and Studies* VI, Cambridge, 1898 and 1904).

Canivet, P., and A. Leroy-Molinghen, ed., *Histoire des moines de Syrie* (Paris, 1977–1979).

Cassola, F., "Aquileia e l'Oriente mediterraneo," *AAAd* 12 (1977), 67–97.

Cavallera, Ferdinand, *Le schisme d'Antioche (IVᵉ–Vᵉ siècle)* (Paris, 1905).

Clark, Elizabeth A., *The Origenist Controversy* (Princeton, 1992).

Croke, Brian, "Arbogast and the Death of Valentinian II," *Historia* 25 (1976), 235–244.

Dattrino, Lorenzo, *Rufino. Storia della chiesa* (Rome, 1986).

Derrett, J. D. M., "The Parable of the Prodigal Son: Patristic Allegories and Jewish Midrashim," *Studia Patristica* 10.1 (Berlin, 1970), 219–224.

Devreesse, Robert, *Le patriarcat d'Antioche* (Paris, 1945).

Di Berardino, Angelo, *Patrology* 4.252 (Westminster, 1991).

Diekamp, Franz, "Gelasius von Caesarea in Palaestina," *Analecta Patristica* (*Orientalia Christiana Analecta* 117 [1938]), 16–49.

Diercks, G. F., ed., *Luciferi Calaritani Opera Quae Supersunt* (CCL 8, 1978).

Dihle, Albrecht, "The Conception of India in the Hellenistic and Roman Literature," *Proceedings of the Cambridge Philological Society* 190 (1964), 15–23.

———, "Umstrittene Daten." *Untersuchungen zum Auftreten der Griechen am Roten Meer* (*Wissenschaftliche Abhandlungen der Arbeitsgemeinschaft für Forschung des Landes Nordrhein-Westfalen* 32 [1965]).

———, "Die entdeckungsgeschichtlichen Voraussetzungen des Indienhandels der römischen Kaiserzeit," *ANRW* II.9.2 (1978), 546–580.

Doignon, Jean, "Hilarius von Poitiers," *RAC* 15 (1991), 139–167.

———, "Palladii de vita Bragmanorum Narratio," *Classica et Medievalia* 21 (1960), 108–135.

Dolzani, C., "Presenze di origine egiziana nell'ambiente aquileiese e nell'alto adriatico," *AAAd* 12 (1977), 125–134.

Dudden, F. H., *The Life and Times of St. Ambrose* (Oxford, 1935).

Duval, Y.-M., "Vrais et faux problèmes concernant le retour d'exil d'Hilaire de Poitiers et son action en Italie en 360–363," *Athenaeum*, n.s., 48 (1970), 251–275.

Engelbrecht, A., ed., *Tyrannii Rufini orationum Gregorii Nazianzeni novem interpretatio* (CSEL 46, 1910).

Engreen, F. E., "The Nilometer in the Serapeum at Alexandria," *Medievalia et humanistica* 1 (1943), 3–13.

Evelyn White, Hugh G., *The Monasteries of the Wâdi 'n Natrûn* (New York, 1932).

Fedalto, Giorgio, "Rufino di Concordia. Elementi di una biografia," *AAAd* 39 (1992), 19–44.

Fedwick, Paul J., "A Chronology of the Life and Works of Basil of Caesarea," in *Basil of Caesarea: Christian, Humanist, Ascetic* (Toronto, 1981), 3–19.

———, *The Church and the Charisma of Leadership in Basil of Caesarea* (Toronto, 1979).

———, ed., *Basil of Caesarea: Christian, Humanist, Ascetic* (Toronto, 1981).

———, "The Translations of the Works of Basil before 1400," in *Basil of Caesarea: Christian, Humanist, Ascetic* (Toronto, 1981), 466–468.

Festugière, A.-J., "Lieux communs littéraires et thèmes de folk-lore dans l'hagiographie primitive," *Wiener Studien* 73 (1960), 123–152.

———, ed., *Historia Monachorum in Aegypto* (Brussels, 1961).

Fischer, Balthasar, "Hat Ambrosius von Mailand in der Woche zwischen seiner Taufe und seiner Bischofskonsekratrion andere Weihen empfangen?," in *Kyriakon, Festschrift Johannes Quasten* (Münster, 1970), 527–531.

Fowden, Garth, "The Last Days of Constantine: Oppositional Versions and Their Influence," *JRS* 84 (1994), 146–170.

Gallay, Paul, *La vie de Saint Grégoire de Nazianze* (Paris, 1943).

Gaudemet, Jean, *L'église dans l'empire romain* (Paris, 1958).

Glas, Anton, *Die Kirchengeschichte des Gelasios von Kaisareia* (*Byzantinisches Archiv* 6, 1914).

Gottlieb, Gunther, "Der Mailänder Kirchenstreit von 385/6," *Museum Helveticum* 42 (1985), 37–55.

Gribomont, J., *Histoire du texte des Ascétiques de S. Basile* (Louvain, 1953).

———, "Notes biographiques sur s. Basile le Grand," in *Basil of Caesarea: Christian, Humanist, Ascetic* (Toronto, 1981), 21–48.

Griffiths, J. G., "Human Sacrifices in Egypt: The Classical Evidence," *Annales du service des antiquités de l'Égypte* 48 (1948), 409–423.

Hammerstaedt, Jürgen, "Hypostasis," *RAC* 16 (1993), 986–1035.

Hammond, C. P., "The Last Ten Years of Rufinus' Life and the date of His Move South from Aquileia," *JTS*, n.s., 28 (1977), 372–429.

Hanson, R. P. C., *The Search for the Christian Doctrine of God* (Edinburgh, 1988).

Heseler, Peter, "Hagiographica I" and "Hagiographica II," *Byzantinisch-Neugriechische Jahrbücher* 9 (1932), 113–128 and 320–337.

Hoffmann, Dietrich, "Wadomar, Bacurius, und Hariulf," *Museum Helveticum* 35 (1978), 307–318.

Honigmann, Ernest, "La liste originale des Pères de Nicée," *Byzantion* 14 (1939), 17–76.

———, "Gélase de Césarée et Rufin d'Aquilée," *Académie royale de Belgique. Bulletin de la classe des lettres et des sciences morales et politiques* 40 (1954), 122–161.

Hübner, Reinhard, *Die Schrift des Apolinarius von Laodicea gegen Photin (Pseudo-Athanasius, contra Sabellianos) und Basilius von Caesarea* (Berlin, 1989).

Jaritz, Horst, "Wasserstandsmessungen am Nil—Nilometer," *Mitteilungen aus dem Leichtweiss-Institut für Wasserbau* 89 (Braunschweig, 1986).

Karayannopoulos, Ioannes, "St. Basil's Social Activity," in *Basil of Caesarea: Christian, Humanist, Ascetic* (Toronto, 1981), 375–391.

Kelly, J. N. D., Early Christian Creeds (London, 1972).

———, *Jerome* (New York, 1975).

Klein, Richard, *Constantius II und die christliche Kirche* (Darmstadt, 1977).

———, "Helena," *RAC* 14 (1988), 355–375.

Kopecek, Thomas A., *A History of Neo-Arianism* (Cambridge, MA, 1979).

Lenox-Conyngham, A. D., "A Topography of the Basilica Conflict of A.D. 385/6 in Milan," *Historia* 31 (1982), 353–363.

———, "Juristic and Religious Aspects of the Basilica Conflict of A.D. 386," *Studia Patristica* 18.1 (1985), 55–58.

Lietzmann, Hans, *Apollinaris von Laodicea und seine Schule* (Tübingen, 1904).

Lordkipanidse, Otar, and Heinzgerd Brakmann, "Iberia II (Georgien)," *RAC* 17 (1995), 12–106.

Maassen, Friedrich, *Geschichte der Quellen und der Literatur des canonischen Rechts* (Gratz, 1870).

Maier, Harry O., "Private Space as the Social Context of Arianism in Ambrose's Milan," *JTS*, n.s., 45 (1994), 72–93.

Mauny, V., "Le Périple de la mer Erythrée et le problème du commerce romain en Afrique au sud du *limes*," *Journal de la Société des Africanistes* 38.1 (1968), 19–34.

Mayerson, Philip, "Mavia, Queen of the Saracens—A Cautionary Note," *Israel Exploration Journal* 30 (1980), 123–131.

Mühlenberg, Ekkehard, *Apollinarius von Laodicea* (Göttingen, 1969).

Murphy, F. X., *Rufinus of Aquileia (345–411): His Life and Works* (Washington, 1945).

Nauroy, Gérard, "Le fouet et le miel. Le combat d'Ambroise en 386 contre l'arianisme milanais," *Recherches augustiniennes* 23 (1988), 3–86.

Orlandi, Tito, *Storia della chiesa di Alessandria* (Milan, 1967).

Ortiz de Urbina, Ignacio, *Nicée et Constantinople* (Paris, 1963).

Palanque, J. R., "Collegialité et partage dans l'empire romain aux IV$^e$ et V$^e$ siècle," *Revue des études anciennes* 46 (1944), 47–64.

Paschoud, François, *Zosime. Histoire nouvelle* (Paris, 1971–1989).

Pellegrino, Michele, *Paolino. Vita di S. Ambrogio* (Rome, 1961).

Piredda, Anna M., "La veste del figliol prodigo nella tradizione patristica," *Sandalion* 8–9 (1985–1986), 203–242.

Pouchet, Robert, *Basile le Grand et son univers d'amis d'après sa correspondance* (Rome, 1992).

Rabe, H. (ed.), *Aphthonii Progymnasmata* (Leipzig, 1926).

———, *Ioannis Sardiani, Commentarium in Aphthonii Progymnasmata* (Leipzig, 1928).

Rives, James B., "Tertullian on Child Sacrifice," *Museum Helveticum* 51 (1994), 54–63.

Rowe, A., "Discovery of the Famous Temple and Enclosure of Serapis at Alexandria," *Supplément aux Annales du Service des Antiquités de l'Égypte*, Cahier 2 (Cairo, 1946).

Rowe, A., and B. R. Rees, "A Contribution to the Archaeology of the Western Desert: IV," *Bulletin of the John Rylands Library* 39.2 (1957), 485–520.

Schamp, Jacques, "Gélase ou Rufin: un fait nouveau," *Byzantion* 57 (1987), 360–390.

———, "The Lost Ecclesiastical History of Gelasius of Caesarea," *The Patristic and Byzantine Review* 6.2 (1987), 146–152.

Schatkin, Margaret A., and Paul W. Harkins, *Saint John Chrysostom Apologist* (*The Fathers of the Church* 73 [1985]).

Scheidweiler, Felix, "Die Kirchengeschichte des Gelasios von Kaisareia," *Byzantinische Zeitschrift* 46 (1953), 277–301.

Schulz-Flügel, Eva (ed.), *Rufinus. Historia Monachorum* (Berlin, 1990).

Schwartz, Eduard, *Gesammelte Schriften* (Berlin, 1938–1963).

Schwartz, Eduard and Theodor Mommsen (ed.), *Eusebius Werke 2.2. Die Kirchengeschichte* (Leipzig, 1908).

Schwartz, Jacques, "La fin du Sérapéum d'Alexandrie," *Essays in Honor of C. Bradford Welles* (New Haven, 1966), 97–111.

Shahîd, Irfan, *Byzantium and the Arabs in the Fourth Century* (Washington, 1984).

Simonetti, Manlio (ed.), *Tyrannii Rufini Opera* (*CCL* 20, 1961).

Spoerl, Kelley M., "The Schism at Antioch since Cavallera," in *Arianism after Arius*, ed. M. R. Barnes and D. H. Williams (Edinburgh, 1993), 101–126.

Stead, Christopher, "Arius in Modern Research," *JTS*, n.s., 45 (1994), 24–36.

Tetz, Martin, "Ein enzyklisches Schreiben der Synode von Alexandrien (362)," *ZNW* 79 (1988), 262–281.

Thelamon, Françoise, *Païens et chrétiens au IV^e siècle* (Paris, 1981).

———, "Rufin historien de son temps," *AAAd* 31 (1987), 1.41–59.

———, "'Apôtres et prophètes de notre temps'," *AAAd* 39 (1992), 171–198.

Vaggione, R. P., *Eunomius: The Extant Works* (Oxford, 1987).

Van Dam, Raymond, "Emperor, Bishops, and Friends in Late Antique Cappadocia," *JTS*, n.s., 37 (1986), 53–76.

Van den Ven, Paul, "Fragments de la recension grecque de l'histoire ecclésiastique de Rufin dans un texte hagiographique," *Le Muséon* 33 (1915), 92–105.

———, "Encore le Rufin grec," *Le Muséon* 59 (1946), 281–294.

Van Roey, A., "Damase," *DHGE* 14 (1960), 48–50.

Williams, Daniel H., "Ambrose, Emperors, and Homoians in Milan: The First Conflict over a Basilica," in *Arianism after Arius*, ed. M. Barnes and D. Williams (Edinburgh, 1993), 127–146.

Williams, Rowan, *Arius* (London, 1987).

Winkelmann, Friedhelm, "Das Problem der Rekonstruktion der Historia Ecclesiastica des Gelasius von Caesarea," *Forschungen und Fortschritte* 38 (1964), 311–314.

———, *Untersuchungen zur Kirchengeschichte des Gelasios von Kaisareia* (*Sitzungsberichte der deutschen Akademie der Wissenschaften zu Berlin*, Klasse für Sprachen, Literatur und Kunst 1965.3).

———, "Charakter und Bedeutung der Kirchengeschichte des Gelasios von Kaisareia," *Byzantinische Forschungen* 1 (1966), 346–385.

———, "Die Quellen der Historia Ecclesiastica des Gelasios von Cyzicus (nach 475)," *Byzantinoslavica* 27 (1966), 104–130.

———, "Zu einer Edition der Fragmente der Kirchengeschichte des Gelasios von Kaisareia," *Byzantinoslavica* 34 (1973), 193–198.

———, "Vita Metrophanis et Alexandri," *Analecta Bollandiana* 100 (1982), 147–184.

Wyss, Bernard, "Gregor von Nazianz," *RAC* 12 (1983), 793–863.

Zecchini, Giuseppe, "Barbari e romani in Rufino di Concordia," *AAAd* 31 (1987), 2.29–60.

Zelzer, Klaus, ed., *Basili Regula* (*CSEL* 86, 1986).

Zintzen, C., ed., *Damascii Vitae Isidori Reliquiae* (Hildesheim, 1967).

## WORKS ON RUFINUS'S TRANSLATIONS

Bammel, Caroline H., "Rufinus' Translation of Origen's Commentary on Romans and the Pelagian Controversy," *AAAd* 39 (1992), 131–149.

Brooks, E. C., "The Translation Techniques of Rufinus of Aquileia (343–411)," *Studia Patristica* 17 (1982), 357–364.

Christensen, Torben, *Rufinus of Aquileia and the "Historia Ecclesiastica," Lib. VIII–IX, of Eusebius* (Copenhagen, 1989).

Crouzel, Henri, "Rufino traduttore del 'Peri Archon' di Origene," *AAAd* 31 (1987), 1.29–39.

Marti, H., "Rufinus' Translation of St. Basil's Sermon on Fasting," *Studia Patristica* 16.2 (1985), 418–422.

Moreschini, Claudio, "Rufino traduttore di Gregorio Nazianzeno," *AAAd* 31 (1987), 227–285.

Oulton, J. E. L., "Rufinus's Translation of the Church History of Eusebius," *JTS* 30 (1929), 150–174.

Pace, Nicola, *Ricerche sulla traduzione di Rufino del "De principiis" di Origene* (Firenze, 1990).

―――, "Un passo discusso della traduzione rufiniana del 'Peri Archon' di Origene," *AAAd* 39 (1992), 199–220.

Simonetti, Manlio, "L'attività letteraria di Rufino negli anni della controversia origeniana," *AAAd* 39 (1992), 89–107.

Wagner, M. M., *Rufinus the Translator* (Washington, 1945).

Winkelmann, Friedhelm, "Einige Bemerkungen zu den Aussagen des Rufinus von Aquileia und des Hieronymus über ihre Übersetzungstheorie und -methode," in *Kyriakon. Festschrift Johannes Quasten*, ed. P. Granfield and J. Jungmann (Münster, 1970), 532–547.

# INDEX OF NAMES

Achillas of Alexandria, successor of
Peter I, 10.1

Aedesius, companion to Frumentius,
10.9

Aetius, teacher of second generation
of Arians, 10.26

Alaric, Gothic leader, Preface

Alexander of Alexandria: dispute
with Arius, 10.1; at Council of
Nicaea, 10.5; rumored to have
banished Arius out of jealousy,
refuses to take him back, 10.12; in
office when Constantius comes to
power, 10.13; death, 10.15; discerns
Athanasius's vocation, 10.15

Alexander of Constantinople: resists
pressure to admit Arius to
communion, 10.13–14

Alexandria: Arius causes dissensions
among Christians of, 10.1; its
bishop has authority over Egypt,

10.6 (VI); Frumentius visits, 10.10;
Arius returns to, 10.12; Alexander
bishop of, 10.13; Athanasius
succeeds Alexander as bishop of,
10.15; festival of Peter Martyr kept
in, 10.15; one of its churches
requested from Athanasius for
Arians, 10.20; George conducts
himself as a tyrant there, 10.24;
Eusebius of Vercelli goes there to
see Athanasius, 10.28; Council of
Alexandria (362), 10.29–30; Tatian
prefect of, 11.2; Lucius seizes see
of, 11.3; news of conversion of
pagans by exiled monks reaches,
11.4; persecution of Nicene
Christians there, 11.6; Moses taken
there for ordination, 11.6; Didymus
teaches there, 11.7; Antony comes
there to support Athanasius, 11.7;
Apollinaris condemned in, 11.20;

Timothy succeeds Peter as bishop of, 11.21; pagan riots, 11.22; destruction of pagan temples of, 11.23–25, 11:28–29; religious reputation of among pagans surpassed by Canopus, 11.26; spared from destruction despite riots, 11.30

Alps, Theodosius crosses, 11.33

Alsa River, Constantine II killed near, 10.16

Ambrose of Milan: elected bishop, 11.11; resists Justina's attempt to appropriate a church, 11.15–16

Andragathius, officer of usurper Maximus: assassinates Gratian, 11.14

Antioch: Athanasius stops there on his return from exile to see Constantius, 10.20; Meletius succeeds to see of, 10.25; Lucifer ordains bishop for, 10.28; divisions among Christians of, 10.31; Daphne suburb of, 10.36; Rufinus sees Theodore in, 10.37; Flavian succeeds Meletius as bishop of, 11.21

Antony, hermit: Constantine writes to, 10.8; his disciples, 11.4; visits Alexandria in support of Athanasius, 11.7; mountain of Antony, 11.8

Apeliotes, place in Egypt, 11.8

Apis, legends about, 11.23

Apollinaris of Laodicea, 11.20

Apollo, Julian consults oracle of in Daphne, 10.36

Aquileia, Constantine II killed not far from, 10.16

Arabia, Mavia attacks settlements on borders of, 11.6

Arbogast: occasions death of Valentinian II, 11.31; commands army of Eugenius, 11.33

Arcadius, son and successor of Theodosius, 11.34

Archelaus, count of Oriens: assists at Council of Tyre (335), 10.17; rescues Athanasius from mob, 10.18

Ariminum, Council of, 10.22, 11.15

Arius, 10.1; opposed by confessors, 10.2; at Council of Nicaea, 10.5; rumored to have aroused Alexander of Alexandria's jealousy, 10.12; recalled by Council of Jerusalem, 10.12; Alexander of Constantinople pressed to receive him, 10.13; his sudden death, 10.14; refused fellowship by his former supporters after his return from exile, 10.26

Armenia, Meletius bishop of Sebaste in, 10.25

Arsenius, lector and alleged victim of Athanasius, 10.16, 10.18

Asterius of Petra, at Council of Alexandria (362), 10.30

Athanasius of Alexandria: at Council of Nicaea, 10.5, 10.15; ordains Frumentius bishop for Aksum, 10.10; his vocation, education, and preparation to succeed Alexander, 10.15; condemned by Council of Tyre, 10.17–18; exile and return, 10.19–20; banished again, 10.20; visited by Eusebius of Vercelli, 10.28; not joined in communion with Meletius of Antioch, 10.31; pursued in vain by Julian, 10.34–35; recalled by Jovian, 11.1; persecution in Egypt starts after his death, 11.2;

his death, 11.3; Didymus greatly in his favor, 11.7; supported by Antony, 11.7; supports Diodore of Tyre, 11.21; safeguards relics of John the Baptist, 11.28

Athens, Gregory and Basil educated there, 11.9

Auxentius of Milan, succeeded by Ambrose, 11.11

Babylas, martyr, his relics silence oracle of Apollo, 10.36

Bacurius, Iberian king and Roman officer, 10.11; distinguishes himself in battle against Eugenius, 11.33

Bartholomew, apostle to Hither India, 10.9

Basil of Caesarea, 11.9

Benivolus, *magister memoriae*, refuses to draft impious law, 11.16

Benjamin, Egyptian hermit, 11.8

Britain, Maximus begins usurpation there, 11.14

[Butheric], officer lynched for refusing to release charioteer, 11.18

Caesarea in Cappadocia, Basil becomes bishop of, 11.9

Canopus, city of magic, 11.26

Cappadocia, 11.9

Carrhae, in Mesopotamia, habitation of monks, 11.8

Castalia, Apollo's spring, 10.36

Cathari, or Novatianists, reception of clergy of, 10.6 (IX)

Cellulae, place in Egypt, 11.8

Chaldaeans, fire-worshipers, 11.26

Christ, Arius departs from faith of, 10.1; philosopher converted to, 10.3; captive converts Georgians by her devotion to, 10.11; Council of

Ariminum asked to choose between *homoousios* and, 10.22

Christians, and holy places, 10.7; in Aksum, 10.9–10; in Georgia, 10.11; Julian's laws against, 10.33; in army, 11.1

Chromatius of Aquileia, Preface

Cilicia, Constantius dies there in Mopsucrenae, 10.27

Constans, emperor: governs West after death of Constantine II, 10.16; receives Athanasius respectfully and forces Constantius to recall him, 10.20; killed by Magnentius, 10.20

Constantia, sister of Constantine and widow of Licinius, persuades her brother to recall Arius, 10.12

Constantine, emperor: summons Council of Nicaea, 10.1; refuses to accept accusations against bishops, 10.2; accepts council's decrees and banishes Arius, 10.5; his mother Helena, 10.7; his piety and victories over barbarians, 10.8; Further India converted to Christianity in his time, 10.9; sends bishops to Georgia, 10.11; recalls Arius, 10.12; his death, 10.12; idolatry begins to fail in his time, 11.19

Constantine II, death of, 10.16

Constantinople, Alexander of, 10.13–14; Macedonius of, 10.26; Macedonian monasteries near, 10.26; Gregory Nazianzen's pastoral work in, 11.9; Apollinaris condemned in, 11.20; Nectarius made bishop of, 11.21

Constantius II: accession, 10.12; Eusebius of Nicomedia's influence over, 10.13; character of, 10.16;

summons Council of Tyre, 10.17; forced by Constans to recall Athanasius, but after Constans's death and defeat of Magnentius persecutes him again, 10.20; his death, 10.27; Liberius returns during his reign, 10.28; careless behavior, 11.1; donates Alexandrian public building to church, 11.22

Cyprus, Spyridon bishop from, 10.5

Cyril of Jerusalem, irregular ordination of, 10.24; predicts failure of project to rebuild Jerusalem temple, 10.38; succeeded by John, 11.21

Damasus of Rome: bloody election of, 11.10; condemns Apollinaris, 11.20; succeeded by Siricius, 11.21

Daphne, suburb of Antioch, 10.36

Didymus the Blind, 11.7

Diodore of Tyre, rejected by Meletius, 11.21

Dionysius of Milan, banished for refusing to condemn Athanasius, 10.21

Edesius. See Aedesius

Edessa: persecution there by Valens, 11.5; monastic settlement, 11.8

Egypt: Paphnutius from, 10.4; subject to bishop of Alexandria, 10.6 (VI); miracles and persecution of monks there, 11.4; monastic settlements, 11.8; failure of paganism in Egypt, 11.22–30

Elijah, monk, 11.8

Elijah, prophet, 11.15

Ethiopia, evangelized by Matthew, 10.9

Eudoxius of Antioch, death of, 10.25

Eugenius, usurper, 11.32–33

Eunomius, leprous Arian leader, 10.26

Eusebius of Caesarea, Preface

Eusebius of Nicomedia: feigns submission to decrees of Nicaea, 10.5; influences Constantius in favor of Arius and presses Alexander of Constantinople to receive him, 10.13–14

Eusebius of Vercelli: banished for refusing to condemn Athanasius, 10.21; exiled to Egypt, 10.28; attends Council of Alexandria (362), 10.29; council's legate to West, 10.30; foiled in attempt to reconcile Antiochene Christians, 10.31; restores to orthodoxy churches of East and of Italy, Illyricum, and Gaul, 10.31–32

Eustathius of Antioch, 10.31

Felix of Rome, succeeds Liberius, 10.23

Flavian (Virius Nicomachus Flavianus), pagan leader during Eugenius's usurpation, 11.33

Flavian of Antioch, succeeds Meletius, 11.21

Foci(?), place in Egypt, 11.8

Frumentius, missionary to Further India, 10.9–10

Galilaeans, Julian's term for Christians, 10.36

Gaul: Julian Caesar in, 10.27; Hilary and Eusebius of Vercelli restore orthodoxy in, 10.32; Valentinian I in, 11.12

George of Alexandria: takes Athanasius's place, 10.20; greed of, 10.24

Georgia, conversion of, 10.11

Goths: attack Italy, Preface;
    Constantine conquers, 10.8; defeat
    and kill Valens, 11.13
Gratian: succeeds Valentinian, 11.12;
    character of, 11.13; death of, 11.14;
    avenged by Theodosius, 11.17
Greeks, legends about Apis, 11.23
Gregory of Alexandria, 10.20
Gregory of Nazianzus, 11.9
Gregory of Nyssa, 11.9

Helena, Constantine's mother: finds
    true cross, 10.7–8; death of, 10.12
Heraclides, Egyptian monk, 11.4
Hiberi. *See* Georgia
Hilary of Poitiers: banished by
    Constantius, 10.21; returns to West
    and restores orthodoxy, 10.31–32
Honorius, appointed emperor of
    West, 11.34

Iberia. *See* Georgia
Illyricum: orthodoxy restored to,
    10.32; Valentinian I dies there,
    11.12
India, conversion of "Further India"
    (Aksum) to Christianity, 10.9–10
Irene, speaks to her father Spyridon
    from the grave, 10.5
Ischyrion, Egyptian monk, 11.8
Isidore, Egyptian monk, 11.4, 11.8
Italy: Alaric invades, Preface; restored
    to orthodoxy, 10.32; its bishops
    reprove Theodosius for ordering
    the massacre at Thessalonica, 11.18

Jerusalem: honors due to bishop of,
    10.6 (VIII); Helena's visit to,
    10.7–8; Bacurius stays with
    Rufinus there, 10.11; Council of
    (335), 10.12; Maximus bishop of,
    10.13; Cyril succeeds Maximus as

bishop of, 10.24; attempt to
    restore temple of, 10.38–40; John
    succeeds Cyril as bishop of, 11.20;
    monastery of Philip in, 11.28
Jesus, 10.3, 10.40, 11.4
Jews, attempt of to rebuild temple in
    Jerusalem, 10.38–40
Jezebel, Justina compared to, 11.15
John, Egyptian monk, consulted by
    Theodosius, 11.19, 11.32
John of Jerusalem, succeeds Cyril,
    11.21
John the Baptist, pagans desecrate
    tomb of, 11.28
Joseph, Egyptian monk, 11.8
Joseph, patriarch, linked with
    Serapis, 11.23
Jovian, emperor, 11.1
Julian, emperor: accession, 10.27–28;
    persecution of Christians, 10.33–37;
    promotes restoration of Jerusalem
    temple, 10.38–40; 11.1, 11.2, 11.28
Julian of Parentium, 11.28
Julius of Rome, succeeded by
    Liberius, 10.23
Jupiter, Serapis assimilated to, 11.23
Justina, mother of Valentinian II,
    supports Arians and attacks
    Ambrose, 11.15–17

Laodicea in Syria, Apollinaris bishop
    of, 11.20
Liberius of Rome: banished, 10.23;
    returns, 10.28; succeeded by
    Damasus, 11.10
Licinius, Constantia widow of, 10.12
Lucifer of Cagliari, banished for
    refusing to condemn Athanasius,
    10.21; ordains Paulinus bishop of
    Antioch, 10.28, 10.31; hesitates to
    accept decisions of Council of
    Alexandria, 10.31

Lucius of Alexandria: seizes see of Alexandria after Athanasius's death and persecutes monks, 11.3–4; Moses refuses to be ordained by, 11.6

Lyons, Gratian assassinated in, 11.14

Macarius, name of two Egyptian monks, 11.4, 11.8

Macarius of Jerusalem, true cross verified by, 10.7–8

Macedonius of Constantinople, heresiarch, 10.26

Magnentius, usurper, kills Constans, 10.20

Mark of Rome, succeeds Silvester, 10.23

Matthew, apostle, missionary to Ethiopia, 10.9

Mavia, Saracen queen, attacks borders of Roman empire, 11.6

Maximian, Caesar and persecutor, 10.4

Maximinus, Flavius, investigates disputed papal election, 11.10

Maximus, usurper, 11.14–17

Maximus of Jerusalem, 10.13; removed from Council of Tyre, 10.18; succeeded by Cyril, 10.24, 10.38

Meletius of Sebaste in Armenia: appointed bishop of Antioch and banished, 10.25; returns, 10.31; succeeded by Flavian, 11.21; refuses to accept Diodore of Tyre, 11.21

Memphis, Apis king of, 11.23

Menelaus, helmsman of, 11.26

Meropius, philosopher, visits India, 10.9

Mesopotamia: Edessa city of, 11.5; monks of, 11.8

Metrodorus, philosopher, visits India, 10.9

Milan, Council of (355), 10.21; Ambrose elected bishop of, 11.11; Justina upsets churches of, 11.15

Mopsucrenae, Constantius dies there, 10.27

Moses, Egyptian monk, 11.8

Moses, monk, ordained bishop of Saracens at Mavia's demand, 11.6

Nazianzus, 11.9

Nectarius of Constantinople, from catechumen to bishop, 11.21

Nicaea, Council of, 10.1–6, 10.15, 10.22

Nicomedia: Eusebius bishop of, 10.5, 10.13; Constantine dies in suburban villa of, 10.12

Nile River, Athanasius flees in boat on, 10.35; Serapis god of, 11.23; Nilometer brought to Serapeum, 11.30

Nitria, place in Egypt, 11.4, 11.8

Novatianists. See Cathari

Olympus, philosopher, leader of pagan uprising in Alexandria, 11.22

Palestine: Bacurius dux limitis in, 10.11; Mavia attacks borders of, 11.6; Sebaste in, 11.28

Pambo, Egyptian monk, 11.4, 11.8

Paphnutius, Egyptian bishop: at Council of Nicaea, 10.4; at Council of Tyre, 10.18

Parentium, Julian bishop of, 11.28

Parthia, evangelized by apostle Thomas, 10.9

Paul, two Egyptian monks of that name, 11.8

Paulianists, or Photinians, rebaptism of, 10.6 (XXI)

Paulinus of Antioch: ordained by Lucifer of Cagliari, 10.28, 10.31;

heads Eustathian party, 10.31;
survives Meletius, 11.21

Paulinus of Trier, banished for
refusing to condemn Athanasius,
10.21

Persia, Julian goes to war against,
10.33, 10.37

Peter I, martyr-bishop of Alexandria,
10.1, 10.15

Peter II: succeeds Athanasius and
flees from Lucius, 11.3; with
Damasus condemns Apollinaris,
11.20; succeeded by Timothy, 11.21

Peter, Basil's brother, 11.9

Philip, apostle, Preface

Philip, Palestinian abbot, sends relics
of John the Baptist to Athanasius,
11.28

Phoci(?). See Foci

Phoenicia, governor of assists at
Council of Tyre, 10.17

Photinians. See Paulianists

Pilate, 10.7

Pispir, place in Egypt, also called
"mountain of Antony," 11.8

Poemen, Egyptian monk, 11.8

Pontus: region of Georgian people,
10.11; Basil evangelizes, 11.9

Probus, Petronius, praetorian prefect,
proclaims Valentinian II emperor,
11.12

Rhodanius of Toulouse, banished for
refusing to condemn Athanasius,
10.21

Romans, barbarians kill them when
they break treaty with Rome, 10.9;
Roman merchants and Christian
liturgy, 10.9, 10.11, 10.12; succession
to Roman empire, 10.12; Roman
people and Liberius, 10.28; Jovian
returns to Roman territory, 11.1;

Mavia wears out Roman army,
11.6; Roman sovereign agrees to
her peace conditions, 11.6;
traditional Roman practice of
government, 11.9; Battle of
Adrianople fatal to Roman
empire, 11.13; punishment of
Roman law for rioting, 11.22

Rome: authority of its bishop in
suburbicarian Italy, 10.6 (VI);
succession of bishops of, 10.23;
Liberius returns to, 10.28; Peter of
Alexandria flees to, 11.3; bloody
papal election in, 11.10;
Theodosius's triumph in, 11.17;
Council of condemns Apollinaris,
11.20; Siricius succeeds Damasus as
bishop of, 11.21; pagans revive
sacrifices in, 11.33

Sabellius, heresy of, 10.30

Salustius. See Salutius

Salutius, Saturninus Secundus,
praetorian prefect under Julian,
tortures the Christian Theodore,
10.37

Samuel, Athanasius compared to,
10.15

Saracens, attack Roman empire, 11.6.
See also Mavia

Sardinia, Lucifer of Cagliari returns
there from exile, 10.31

Sarmatians: Constantine defeats, 10.8;
Valentinian sets out against, 11.12

Saturn, temple of in Alexandria place
of debauchery, 11.24–25

Scete, place in Egypt, 11.8

Scyrion. See Ischyrion

Sebaste in Armenia, Meletius bishop
of, 10.25

Sebaste in Palestine, burial place of
John the Baptist, 11.28

Seleucia, Council of, 10.22

Serapis: temple of in Alexandria, 11.23; views concerning, 11.23; site of temple of used for church, 11.27; busts of destroyed, 11.29; Nilometer brought to temple of, 11.30

Sicininus, Ursinus irregularly ordained bishop of Rome in basilica of, 11.10

Silvester of Rome, succeeded by Mark, 10.23

Siricius of Rome, succeeds Damasus, 11.21

Spyridon of Trimithus, at Council of Nicaea: miraculously fastens thieves to his sheep pen, asks his dead daughter about a deposit, 10.5

Tatian (Flavius Eutolmius Tatianus), prefect of Egypt under Valens and persecutor of orthodox, 11.2

Thebaid, monastic settlement at, 11.7, 11.19

Theodore, tortured by Salutius (q.v.), 10.37

Theodosius: appointed emperor by Gratian, 11.14; avenges him, 11.17; orders massacre in Thessalonica, 11.18; character of, 11.19; donates public building in Alexandria to bishop, 11.22; leniency toward Alexandrian rioters, 11.22; relief of that Alexandria spared from destruction, 11.30; war against Eugenius, 11.31–33; death and succession, 11.34

Theophilus of Alexandria: succeeds Timothy, 11.21; receives disused building from Theodosius for church, 11.22; destroys temple of Canopus, 11.26

Thessalonica, massacre in following lynching of Butheric (q.v.), 11.18

Thomas, apostle: missionary to Parthia, 10.9; relics of kept in Edessa, 11.5

Thrace, Goths invade, 11.13

Timothy, presbyter of Athanasius, helps reveal false accusation at Council of Tyre, 10.18

Timothy of Alexandria, succeeds Peter II, 11.21

Tyrannus, priest of Saturn, his crimes revealed, 11.25

Tyre: Meropius from, 10.9; Aedesius from, 10.10; Council of, 10.17–18; schism in, 11.21

Ursinus, antipope, irregular ordination of, 11.10

Valens, appointed emperor of East: persecutes orthodox, 11.2, 11.5; agrees to Mavia's request for ordination of Moses, 11.6; cancels order for Basil's exile when his son dies, 11.9; belated repentance and death in battle, 11.13

Valentinian I: proclaimed emperor, 11.2; careful administration, 11.9; confirms Ambrose's election, 11.11; death, 11.12

Valentinian II: proclaimed co-emperor with Gratian while quite young, 11.12–13; feigns peace treaty with Maximus, 11.15; sends troops to arrest Ambrose, 11.15; flees before Maximus's advance, 11.16; restored by Theodosius, 11.17; death, 11.31

Venus, image of erected by pagans on site of Christ's crucifixion, 10.7